THE LISTENER'S GUIDE TO

Great Instrumentalists

by

DAVID HAMILTON

Facts On File

A Quarto Book
Copyright © by Quarto Marketing Ltd. and David Hamilton

First published in the United States in 1982 by **Facts On File, Inc.**

Library of Congress Cataloging in Publication Data
Hamilton, David, 1935–
   The listener's guide to great instrumentalists.
   Discography.
   1. Instrumental music—Discography. 2. Music—Performance—
   Discography. 3. Music—Interpretation (Phrasing, dynamics,
   etc.) 4. Virtuosity in music.
I. Title.
ML156.4.158H35   780'.1'5   81-9811
ISBN 0-87196-568-2   AACR2

The Listener's Guide to Great Instrumentalists was produced and
prepared by Quarto Marketing Ltd.
212 Fifth Avenue, New York, N.Y. 10010

The Listener's Guide Series was conceived by John Smallwood

Editor: Gene Santoro
Designer: Elizabeth Fox
Typesetting: Scarlett Letters Inc. N.Y.
Printed and Bound in the United States
by the Maple Vail Group

PREFACE

Although this book is intended as a general introduction to the art of the solo instrumentalist and to the literature for the major solo instruments, I have chosen the specific examples from among recordings made during the years before and just after World War II. This is not because I think there have been no great instrumentalists since 1950—far from it. But I presume that most readers who have begun to explore classical music have done so through recent recordings, live concerts, or television. Though this exposes them to a certain range of styles of performance, records in fact make it possible to hear a still greater range, to revisit earlier eras and hear how people of those times played—and understood—the same musical works that are played today, sometimes in perceptibly different ways.

Despite changes of musical taste and our increased historical knowledge about how music of the past was played in its own day, older recordings still have things to tell us. Recorded sound may have made absolute progress over the last century, but when applied to musical understanding and interpretation, "progress" is a more questionable concept. At the least, these older performances give us a new perspective on the way modern performers play, setting into relief the mannerisms that we tend to take for granted; thus, they tell us something about ourselves and our taste as well.

The basis of the book is a selection of twenty-five recordings, mostly single disks but including several boxed sets of considerable substance and value. The list of recordings should not be taken as an honor roll of "the best recordings of the century," or even a list of my personal favorites. Since the book is addressed principally to beginning collectors, I felt that the emphasis must be on recordings that can be readily acquired, not on long-out-of-print rarities that turn up only in the second-hand market at premium prices, or can be heard only in sound archives. Every recording featured in the book is, at the time of writing, currently available in either the United States or the United Kingdom (or both), either locally produced or circulating as an import—and the presumption is that what is available on one side of the Atlantic can be obtained on the other, if a little less readily. (The same does not hold for the Pacific; I have ignored the vast Japanese catalogues of historical reissues, since the records are only rarely to be found in the US and UK, and then only in small quantities and at high prices. See Appendix B for information about obtaining imported recordings.) In some instances, I have supplied French or German catalogue numbers as well as US and UK ones, for sometimes the European editions turn out to be more readily available.

Many significant and treasurable recordings will therefore not be found among the featured items here. At the end of each entry, a brief survey of the performer's other recordings calls attention not only to those currently available, but also to those now out-of-print, against the likelihood that sooner or later they may be returned to the active lists. Historical reissues come and go in waves, often in connection with birthdays and anniversaries. In 1973, for example, RCA honored the Rachmaninoff centennial by rereleasing all of his recordings—but most of that series has now vanished. Solomon is very "available" right now, and Adolf Busch's recordings are being resuscitated in quantity by EMI in Britain. The moral of the story is to grab historical reissues when they turn up, as they tend to be short-lived.

The fact that this is an introductory book also suggested the exclusion of acoustical recordings (pre-1925), except for a few individual tracks inextricably combined with electricals on recital collections (for example, Rachmaninoff and Kreisler). Although important instrumental and even orchestral recordings were made during the acoustical period, there is no doubt that a certain effort and experience are required from the listener to extract the historical information they contain, let alone the aesthetic pleasure. After hearing a few acoustical recordings by Kreisler and Rachmaninoff, you may be sufficiently intrigued to look into others, and of course there are many fabled performers who did not live long enough to record by the electrical process, or were too old to do themselves justice by 1925.

At the other end, the time limit has been a little more flexible; the featured recordings of Dennis Brain and William Primrose and some of the Horowitz selections were originally taken down on tape in the early 1950s, but as far as I know almost everything else stems from disk originals—mostly 78 RPM studio recordings and a few transcriptions from concert performances. The omission of some notable performers who were active during the period 1925–1950 does not necessarily indicate a lack of admiration for their work (although it may). For some, no representative recordings are readily available right now, or at least none from the appropriate period. A case in point: Artur Rubinstein, who recorded for HMV in the 1930s and Victor in the 1940s, continued to record—and rerecord—his repertoire through the LP and stereo eras, right into the 1970s, with the consequence that few of his early recordings have been reissued, and in most cases the later ones are superior anyway.

The sequence of the recordings within the main sections of the book, which may at first appear somewhat random, has been devised with the novice listener in mind, proceeding from shorter to longer works, introducing the instruments and their technical features as well as the musical forms written for them. Naturally, a book such as this cannot constitute a systematic introduction to music, its history, and its composers, but I have at least tried to suggest the important concepts, to call attention to some aspects of performance that may not be immediately obvious. Not even the most eloquent description is an adequate substitute for actually hearing a musical performance, and I have not sought to provide such substitutes, but rather to furnish information, impressions, indications that, *in conjunction with the sounds on the recordings*, may lead to appreciation of the special qualities of the great instrumentalists of years past.

My thanks to John Smallwood and Gene Santoro of Quarto, who interested me in the project and, by judicious application of carrot and stick, kept my nose to the grindstone. Also to Judith Stein for her speedy and accurate preparation of the manuscript. My oldest debt of gratitude in connection with this book is to two colleagues, David Hall and Irving Kolodin, in the pages of whose books about recorded music I first encountered most of the recordings celebrated herein.

New York
July 1981

David Hamilton

1

THE ART OF THE INSTRUMENTALIST

A musical performer engages simultaneously in several activities. Although, as with any such abstract schematization, the boundaries are not always clear-cut, we might distinguish three such activities: execution, interpretation, and projection. They relate, respectively, to the instrument, the musical work, and the listener. The performer must have sufficient command of the instrument to execute the music that has been written for it. He must understand the piece he is playing, must have (at least instinctively, not necessarily in a verbally articulate form) a conception of its shape and its sense. And finally, he must communicate that conception, and a sense of his own involvement in the whole process, to the audience.

The relative importance of these three activities is by no means constant. Some performers are natural showmen, gifted at projecting themselves and what they are doing. Others are principally musical thinkers, with exceptionally sharp perceptions about the works they are playing. Not only do players differ; particular musical works call for differing proportions of these attributes. Some music does not require sharp perceptions or deep insights, for it was written primarily to show off the performer's command of the instrument, his graceful phrasing and vivid personality (such pieces are, not surprisingly, most often written by composers who are themselves performers). At another extreme there is music that was originally intended as much for the performer's private enjoyment as for projection to an audience—for example, much of the keyboard music of Bach, written for domestic and pedagogical use in an era when the public concert was scarcely known. Today, of course, such music is often played in concert halls, and must necessarily be projected in a way that its composer can hardly have contemplated.

In the long run, most of us would probably prefer to spend our listening time with illuminating performances of the greatest works of the literature, but there are also pleasures and values associated with lesser works and their performance, pleasures and values that may also help the listener to discern the special qualities of great performers. The swelling waves of sound that a master pianist such as Vladimir Horowitz can draw from his instrument can have an aesthetic value of their own, independent of the value of the music being played.

Playing the Instrument

The first of the performer's three activities is playing his instrument—mastering its technique, becoming a virtuoso. To most of us, the word virtuosity initially summons up images of velocity and volume: the ability to play very many notes very quickly, the ability to extract a full, rich sound from the instrument. But that is a narrow definition. True technical command involves less obvious accomplishments as well. Tonal quality, of course: avoiding the ugly noises of which every instrument is capable, commanding the various possibilities of timbre (tone color) that it offers, bringing each to its optimum quality. To play very softly yet still firmly, to utter a long phrase without a break or loss of tension may require a control of breath or muscle quite as demanding as playing at lightning speed.

Central to the highest virtuosity is the matter of articulation—the many ways in which a single note may be begun and ended, approached and left. Different instruments naturally offer different possibilities. The violin, like the human voice, can slide from one note to the next, filling in the gap between—but the piano cannot. Both strings and winds can swell on a note after it has begun; the piano cannot. Some instruments "speak" easily; in others, a certain amount of inertia must be overcome before the sound will start, and so a quiet attack is not easy. The number of gradations a player can produce between sharp *staccato* (detached) and fully *legato* (tied) articulations, the facility with which he can move among the different possibilities available on his instrument—these give his playing a potential range of light and shade, of dimension and depth, of variety and specificity.

Often, though not always, this complex of skills called virtuosity is a consequence of unusual natural endowments—not only physical ones, such as hands of a particular size and shape, but also invisible attributes such as coordination, the reflexes and responses that are also found in great athletes. The great musical athlete has exceptional endowment in another faculty as well: the ear. The physical potential of hands, arms, lips, or lungs needs the guidance of an ear that can distinguish the finest shades of pitch, color, and articulation, and can recall them as needed from the body and the instrument. Equally important, that ear must be quick to detect inadvertent emphases or unevennesses in the playing, to prevent the development of involuntary mannerisms.

Interpreting the Notation

Interpretation is a complex concept, operating at several levels. The first of these entails the most literal meaning of the word, for the performer has to interpret the musical notation, the written symbols used by the composer. This does not mean just the simple skill of reading music—performers learn that very early. However, musical notation has not remained a language of fixed meaning over the many centuries during which pieces have been written down. At different times and places, the same symbol may have represented different things, or the same thing may have been represented by different symbols. In the past, music was often written principally for performance by, or under the direct supervision of, its composer, and many local conventions and common practices were not even written down; they were either taken for granted or transmitted by word of mouth. Sometimes, where notation was imprecise or where modern scholarship has been unable to unearth independent information, we simply do not know how a certain detail may have been played. There are cases, too, where a composer did not make up his mind, leaving contradictory indications, and the performer will thus have to make it up for him.

Until well into the 18th century, the performance of anything except contemporary music was very unusual, so it didn't occur to composers to worry about making things clear to posterity; they had no reason to believe posterity would be much interested. But as the performance of "the classics" began to occupy an ever larger part of concert life, composers realized that their music might have a greater life expectancy than they themselves; in the hope that they, too, would become classics, they put ever more specific instructions in their scores for future interpreters. Performers became accustomed to this wealth of detailed indications, and came to suppose that all scores, from all periods, were meant to be followed as religiously as the newest ones. This development had the unfortunate effect of suppressing such quite sound traditional conventions as still survived. Over the past century, historical scholarship has gradually filled out our knowledge of what *isn't* in the score; we now know, for example, that a good deal of music from the 18th century was written with the expectation that the performer would improvise variations on it, and that playing "exactly what is written" is the last thing the composer would have wanted. Modern scholarship has also made available to performers more accurate and more informative editions of the music of the past.

Still, literal adherence to the score, even where it is appropriate, is necessarily something of an illusion, for the symbols of musical notation are relatively crude. This applies even to pitch, which a good singer or instrumentalist (though not a keyboard player) can "bend" to emphasize a melodic tendency. Modern notation has ways of specifying this, but most composers have simply left it up to the taste and skill of the performer. Similarly, though the symbols for relative duration of notes are precise, a mechanically accurate realization of that precision would sound stiff and inhuman. (Sometimes, the nature of the appropriate deviations is a matter of tradition as well as of individual discretion—for example, in dance styles such as the Viennese waltz.)

The composer may have indicated the speed of his music by a metronome marking, specifying the number of beats per minute, but more than a few have suggested that these numbers are meant only as general directions; factors such as room acoustics, for example, may encourage considerable deviation (you may have to play more slowly in a very resonant room). The fact that composers such as Brahms and Wagner—who could well have supplied metronome marks—did not do so, suggests that they did not wish to confine the performer too strictly. The metronome marks of Beethoven, one of the first composers to use the then-new device, are in fact often disregarded, on the grounds that the deaf composer set improbable tempos based on running through his earlier works in his head rather than actually playing them; at the least, some of his marks seem to have been garbled in transmission. Prior to the 19th century, we find only the most general indications: Allegro, Presto, Andante, Adagio, and the like.

By the same token, however carefully a composer may indicate the dynamics and articulations he wishes, the symbols available for the task are crude by comparison with the gradations a good player can produce. (A player-piano manufacturer, trying to persuade Artur Schnabel to record piano rolls for his instrument, boasted that it could reproduce "sixteen nuances, from pianissimo to fortissimo." "Too bad," replied the waggish pianist, "*I* happen to use seventeen.") Thus the composer's score, even as supplemented by the best historical knowledge, really only defines a range of possibilities, within which the performer must make his own decisions.

Interpreting the Music

To characterize another level of interpretation, it is profitable to draw an analogy with the actor's task. His lines and stage directions are but the surface manifestations of a character, yet from them the actor must construct in his mind a complete person who is consistent with that given surface; once he has constructed such a person, he has a basis upon which to decide precisely how to read the lines (which words to stress, how quickly to speak, and so forth), and how to carry out the stage directions (whether to exit left with a confident stride or to skulk away, for example). So, just as the actor forms a conception of the person he is acting, the musician forms a conception of a piece, digging beneath the written notes to discover its structure, its expressivity—its meaning.

Form and Structure

The structure of every musical work is unique, although it may well share patterns and procedures with other works. The standard musical forms, such as sonata-allegro, rondo, and theme-and-variations, are textbook abstractions from the common practice of many composers; what is distinctive about a particular work is, as a rule, the ways it departs from standard formulas, the things that happen over and above the common procedures. These stereotypes of form are, nevertheless, useful to both performer and listener as starting points, general indications of what to expect, backgrounds against which unexpected events will stand out.

The most complex and important of these standard patterns is Classical sonata-allegro form, which in one variety or another dominates most of the music considered in this book. It usually entails the exposition of two principal groups of contrasting thematic material in two contrasting keys (the tonic and, generally, its closest relative, the fifth degree, known as the dominant); the development—fragmentation, extension, transformation, or combination—of these themes; and the recapitulation, or return to the tonic key, in which the themes are restated and a conclusion reached. Other common forms involve simpler repetitions of sections, alternations of contrasting material, or systematic variation of a single theme. In all such contexts, repetition and variation of thematic material entails consistent and logical articulation by the performer, so that the connections are not obscured but rather, if possible, clarified. Repeated material does not have to be always phrased the same way—but if he is altering its phrasing, the player should be doing it consciously and know *why* he is doing it.

Basic to the understanding of musical structure is an awareness that, although many pieces appear to share the same form, each uses the common patterns in its unique way. In a Haydn movement, for example, the same melodic idea may serve as both first and second theme, so that the principal tension of the piece is a harmonic one, arising from the contrast of tonic and dominant keys, from the movement away from, and eventually back to, the home key. Schubert, on the other hand, is fond of ranging about harmonically for expressive purposes in the presentation of his themes; since this tends to dilute the effect of the harmonic contrasts that Haydn exploited, Schubert compensates with highly contrasted themes—sometimes so disparate, in fact, that it is hard to find a single tempo in which both of them feel comfortable. (In such a situation, the performer has to decide which matters more, the individual expressivity of the themes or the unity of the movement's tempo—or whether he can perhaps make smooth, subtle adjustments of tempo so that both themes find their best speed without apparent loss of tension or continuity.)

Thus, the same ostensible form may harbor radically different works, divergent in dimension or emphasis. In the *Goldberg Variations*, Bach systematically erects a series of elaborations on the bass line (and harmonies) of his theme, while in the *Diabelli Variations*, Beethoven concentrates successively on each aspect, each element of his theme; these two monumental examples of variation form are in fact complementary rather than similar. Although in symphonies and sonatas of the 18th century the greatest weight is almost always in the first movement, Beethoven begins to upset that by experimenting with novel cycles of movements, often interrelated and coming to a resolution of some sort only in the finale—and with that the door is open to many possibilities. The performer must decide whether—and where—the tension accumulates or dissipates in a piece or a cycle of pieces—and upon the resulting conception will depend even such matters as the length of the pauses between movements.

Symmetry and expectation play an important role in music, especially that of the Classical period. A norm of four-measure phrases, usually in pairs (in the complementary relation known as "antecedent and consequent") is characteristic, standing in the background even of many phrases that do not come out "even" but which are in fact extensions, contractions, or overlapping combinations of regular phrases. Composers play with the listener's expectations, building them up and then deceiving them for humorous or dramatic effect. A performer insensitive to the background, the pattern against which such events develop, will likely obscure them.

Matters of musical style and structure have a bearing on the treatment of tempo, as well. Prior to the middle of the 19th century, most pieces, or their individual movements, were in a single meter and tempo; any changes (for example, after a slow introduction, or in theme-and-variation sequences) were made cleanly and clearly. Later, tempo transitions became a regular resource of the musical language, in Liszt's symphonic poems with sections in different tempos, in his Piano Sonata with its four-movements-folded-into-one structure, and in Wagner's operas. Still later, in the 20th century, composers began to use rapidly changing meters in the same tempo. In each of these situations, any ongoing modification of the tempo has a different effect on the listener's perception of the music. Some freedom with the pulse of a Beethoven slow movement, to emphasize a structural event or an expressive point, is not likely to obscure the straightforward meter, but the sense of a Wagnerian tempo transition will probably be undermined if it does not flow from and to rather steady pulses—and any variation at all of the pulse of the "Sacrificial Dance" that ends Stravinsky's *The Rite of Spring* will quickly render it incoherent.

Expressive Character

Hard to define, harder to describe, and still harder to argue about, is the expressive aspect of music. Philosophers have debated the hows and whys of musical meaning for centuries, but in practice most musicians simply take that meaning for granted, and don't waste much time trying to find verbal equivalents for the expressive character of a piece; as Mendelssohn once argued, the meaning of music is actually more specific than that of words. In his study and analysis of a piece, the performer arrives at a conception of its character as well as of its structure—indeed, the two are inextricably interwoven. Shorter and simply structured pieces often present a single character or a direct contrast, but long and complex pieces pass through many phases, each of which must be articulated as distinctively as possible.

Sometimes the demands of notation, structure, and character appear to be in conflict, and the performer must try to reconcile them, searching for an interpretation that will accommodate them all. (Another Schnabel anecdote suggests how that process might work: when a pupil asked him, "Is it better to play in time or to play as you feel?" Schnabel replied, "Why not feel in time?") Just as we expect the structure of a piece to be coherent in performance, so too do we expect a coherent character, not a hodge-podge, disjointed and spastic in its expressivity. And we respond most strongly to performances that make each phase of a work's expressive progress as vivid, as characterful as possible.

The Importance of Rhythm

In defining both structure and character, the musical dimension that most concerns the performer is rhythm, that nexus on which converge meter, pulse, accent, tempo, rate of harmonic and textural change, even dynamics and phrasing. The interrelationships among these elements are complex, and our understanding of their relative functions is more intuitive than systematic, but they constitute, literally, the heartbeat of music. Rhythm, the actual progression of music in real time, is the special responsibility of the performer to realize in sound, through the use of hundreds of small, subtle, mostly intuitive adjustments and enhancements of the literal indications of the score. If a melody is rhythmically ambiguous, at what point, if ever, should its meter be clarified? Does the principal stress come at the beginning of the phrase or at the end—or should there be no conspicuous stress at all? Should an unexpected harmonic shift be underlined by dynamics, or by tempo, or by neither? Where are the big downbeats in a movement, the long-range points of arrival, and how should they be prepared and emphasized? A piece may have a very busy foreground activity and yet relatively slow harmonic motion—what should be the proper emphases to keep each level moving?

The Interpreter's Role

Such questions only hint at the range of decisions a player must make, consciously or intuitively. They also suggest the inappropriateness of many generalizations about the "right" way to play music—indeed, even of generalizations about works that are superficially quite similar. There is music designed to accommodate the idiosyncrasies and technical achievements of performers, music that will bend to fit strong individual personalities (a good deal of popular music is explicitly, and very skillfully, designed to just this end). But the greatest pieces acquire their fullest significance only when their unique qualities are realized and projected. One of the characteristics often ascribed to great music is inexhaustibility, the number of different ways in which its uniqueness can be realized—and it seems probable that some great and complex works can never be completely realized in a single performance.

In practice, some performers bring a single approach, a limited set of mannerisms and stock responses, to the majority of the pieces they play. Yet even such players sometimes encounter a piece that happens to match their mannerisms and personalities perfectly. But most of the time it is the others, the performers with the greatest variety of resources, the most specific responses to individual pieces, whose every concert and recording we search out. Heifetz's sheer fiddling is never without interest, for example, but he has rarely surprised me with an unexpected and significant gesture in a Beethoven sonata; on the other hand, every recording Schnabel ever made, no matter how wrong-headed it might be in some respect, contains insights that I could never have foreseen.

To sum up, the interpreter's task could be defined as that of constructing a three-dimensional reality in sound and time from the flat and incomplete information supplied by the printed page, a reality that should be internally coherent as well as consistent with the limits defined by the printed page and by historical knowledge about the work, the composer, and the period. As already suggested, a certain amount of that reality must necessarily be speculative, but the extent of this no-man's-land will vary depending on the nature of the piece, its balance between the structural and expressive aspects, its historical and national origins, even its form and genre.

Adherents of the doctrine of "playing just what is in the score" prefer to whittle down that speculative area as much as possible, while others seek to enlarge it, to give the performer more scope for his personality. The tension between these two points of view has long been a feature of the musical landscape, and in truth it is a fruitful tension, each extreme acting as a brake on the other. Towards the middle of the 20th century, the literalists may have been markedly in the ascendance (at least in the US and UK, where Toscanini and Schnabel were the most influential interpreters), but that is no longer necessarily so. Today we would probably not allow a performer to go as far as, say, Rachmaninoff was once permitted to go in stretching, even altering, a composer's explicit instructions (and implicit conception of his work), but such things are always ultimately subject to the conviction and authority of the performer. Even among literalists, few will deny the effectiveness of Rachmaninoff's interpretation of the Chopin Sonata in B-flat minor (to be discussed below), no matter how arbitrarily it deals with the printed score.

Projection

This brings us to the third of the performer's tasks, projection. In addition to knowing and understanding the piece and executing it proficiently, the performer must be able to bring the piece to life again and again, as if freshly minted. He must be able to convince us that this music—this experience—is happening right now, especially and uniquely for us. His success in this hinges in part on our sense of his personal commitment to the piece and to his conception of it; he must in some degree project himself as well as the music.

Sometimes we may feel that he is projecting more of himself than of the music, perhaps even rendering the music incoherent in the process. A possible metaphor is that of hand and glove: the performer's hand should fit the composer's glove amply, but without rending it. If the fit is good, the hand will remain identifiable as its owner's, for it will have subtly affected the shape of the glove. As in other aspects of interpretation, there is no single correct proportion, but, rather, a wide continuum between a passive, uncommitted reading and an overly personal act of aggression that demolishes that piece.

The Performer and the Phonograph

Since the beginning of the 20th century, nearly all of the great musical performers have made recordings. The relatively primitive acoustical method of recording in use before 1925 was much more sympathetic to voices than to instruments, so the emphasis in those years was on opera and song. Though there are also intriguing souvenirs of composer-pianists such as Grieg and Debussy, of violinists such as Sarasate and Brahms's friend Joachim, these are restricted to short pieces that would fit the four-minute time span of a 78 RPM record side. After 1925, when the introduction of electrical recording techniques allowed much greater fidelity of instrumental reproduction and a wider dynamic range, substantial works—symphonies, sonatas, concertos, quartets—began to be recorded by the leading instrumentalists and conductors of the day. Eventually, in 1948, the introduction of the long-playing record dramatically reduced the physical bulk and manufacturing cost of recorded music, and did away with the tiresome and mood-destroying interruptions every four minutes or so for record-changing.

Today, in stereophonic sound and with the latest techniques of digital mastering, leading performers continue to make recordings of the standard musical literature, and the range of musical repertoire available on records has increased beyond any bounds imaginable a half-century ago. In 1930, Machaut and Monteverdi were but names in music history books; now we can choose among multiple recordings of their works. Only the most celebrated contemporary works were recorded back then; today, we can study and become familiar with the music of hundreds of living composers. Even the musics of non-Western cultures, albeit torn from the cultural contexts that may be an indispensable part of their significance, can be heard in our living rooms.

Despite the remarkable richness and realistic sound of current recordings, however, earlier ones continue to be reissued and listened to—many of them now well over a half-century old. Why is this so? Why should people be willing to tolerate surface scratch, limited frequency range, and other sonic limitations when the same musical works are available in versions boasting almost uncanny tonal accuracy, natural concert-hall ambience, and noise-free backgrounds?

The Value of Older Recordings

There are a number of reasons, all related to one central fact: these performances from the past are different from those of today, different in ways that cannot now be duplicated. An obvious kind of difference is clearest in the case of singers, for their very instruments are quite literally unique—nobody can imitate the sound of a Caruso or a Flagstad. And, just as singing involves a unique instrument, it may also involve an exceptionally vivid projection of personality; although we may never have laid eyes on Lotte Lehman or Ezio Pinza, we can feel that we know them personally from their recordings.

Similar personal characteristics mark the work of fine instrumental players, though to a degree less immediately obvious: a particular combination of physique, instrument, technique, and musical approach results in a very distinctive sound. It is impossible to confuse the silken suavity of Fritz Kreisler's fiddling with the hotter vibrance of Heifetz's tone, let alone the more wiry intensity of Szigeti. And, as with singers, the combination of tonal quality and musical style can delineate a personality so vividly that we feel in direct human contact. Thus, the unique sound and personality of exceptional individuals lives on in their recordings.

Composers' Recordings

Another reason an older recording may still be consulted is that the performer can claim special authority: the composer, perhaps, or the player for whom the piece was written or to whom it was dedicated or who gave the first performance. Recordings in this category are seldom devoid of interest, although they are by no means necessarily enjoyable, or even convincing, coherent, or accurate performances. Some composers—for example, Rachmaninoff—have also been great performers, but for others performance (usually conducting) has been a secondary occupation, a skill acquired later in life and then often imperfectly. Still, a composer may know a lot about his own piece, may have very definite ideas about how it should go, and may be sufficiently accomplished to project those ideas in performance.

But whether those recordings should be accorded a special position as a criterion against which all other performances are measured is a highly debatable point. For one thing, there's a good deal of evidence to suggest that most composers, far from thinking in terms of a single definitive performance, instead relish the variety of interpretations that result when different gifted individuals play their music. Rachmaninoff, for example, admired the quite personal performances of his Third Piano Concerto given by Vladimir Horowitz, and we will encounter, in our discussion of Elgar's Violin Concerto, a similar case of quite disparate interpretations, both enthusiastically approved by the composer.

Furthermore, it is worth considering the possibility that a composer may not necessarily understand all the implications of his own work, especially when he is a stylistic innovator. Béla Bartók was indubitably a great pianist as well as a great composer, but he was a pianist trained before the turn of the century who played with some of the stylistic habits of that period, one of which was a tendency to "roll" chords from the bottom up rather than playing all the notes simultaneously. In 19th-century music, this rarely obscures the regular metrical patterns, but Bartók also does it in his own music, where the asymmetrical and irregular rhythms surely need to be sharply and unequivocally articulated. (Rachmaninoff, on the other hand, composed in the old-fashioned style of the period he grew up in, and so the old-fashioned features of his playing are perfectly appropriate.)

A sensible attitude towards composer performances would be one of respectful attention rather than abject submission; even the finest of them (such as the Menuhin/Elgar recording) represent only one of many potential ways to play a piece, not a dogmatic assertion of a "right" way. And the same is true for recordings by performers closely associated with the composer, or those who took part in the first performance. For my own part, I have attended enough first performances during the last several decades to know that first is rarely best, and is sometimes worst—or so the suffering composer must devoutly hope.

Historical Authenticity

This question is, of course, an aspect of the larger one of authenticity. The growth of musical-historical scholarship has in recent years brought to the fore the doctrine that one of the tasks of performance is to reproduce the conditions of the composer's time and place. Occasionally this is stated as if the ideal were actually to reconstruct the work's first performance—often a questionable ideal, as I have just suggested. But what the more sophisticated adherents of historicism in performance essentially advocate is the reconstruction of the best possible contemporary conditions: the best players using the best instruments that would have been known to the composer, aware of the appropriate performance conventions, playing in a room of appropriate size.

Earlier stages of this movement are represented in the Bach recordings of Wanda Landowska and Adolf Busch discussed in this book, but its most far-reaching developments have come since 1960, with the increased use of period instruments (or reconstructions and copies of them). This has introduced a fascinating range of new possibilities in the performance of earlier music, but it does not necessarily invalidate the musical virtues of older, less historically accurate approaches. (Landowska's Pleyel may have been a hopelessly inauthentic hybrid, but even the most scholarly of today's harpsichordists still envies her technique, rhythm, musicianship, and imagination.)

Indeed, one of the fascinations of older recordings is the insight they give about how an earlier generation perceived music that we now hear somewhat differently. Busch's Bach, for example, with its concentration on contrapuntal clarity, phrasing, and rhythmic vitality, reflects the musical interests of the era of Brahms and Max Reger; today's performances assign relatively greater weight to tone color—not surprising in a period when composers have often elevated tone color to a structural role in their music. It wouldn't surprise me, either, to find that in another thirty or forty years Bach will be played in still another way, and that today's "authentic" performances will be recognized as very much a product of their own time.

Authenticity and Local Traditions

Another aspect of authenticity is the idea that music is best interpreted by compatriots of the composer. This, too, should be examined and treated with some care. Undeniably, there are—or, at any rate, *were,* before the musical world reached its present condition of internationalization—distinctive local traditions of technique, training, and interpretation. The Franco-Belgian school of violinists learned to play the violin in much the same way as had the violinist-composers Vieuxtemps and Ysaÿe, as the violinists for whom French composers of the later 19th century wrote their music. This style of playing was very different from that of the German school, epitomized by Joseph Joachim, first interpreter of Brahms's Violin Concerto. A background of shared musical tradition hardly guarantees a good performance, of course, but it may well give a performer a head start, because he is more likely than a player from another tradition to have spent his formative years in contact with stylish and understanding performances of the music.

At the same time, a performer without that head start—and thus without any preconceptions—might be stimulated to come up with an original and powerful interpretation. A good example is Joseph Szigeti's imaginative performance of Prokofiev's First Violin Concerto, a work calling for sounds produced in unconventional ways. Violinists trained to the Russian ideal of rich beautiful violin tone went along grudgingly with these demands, but Szigeti, drawing on his Hungarian background and its tradition of freewheeling gypsy fiddling, enthusiastically cooperated with Prokofiev, giving the whole work a novel yet coherent tonal color.

When it comes to music in which nationalistic elements—especially subtle rhythmic inflections and freedom of tempo—play a prominent role, it probably does help to have grown up in the right country. That's especially true of vocal music, where the rhythm may derive from the rhythm of the words themselves, but instrumental music, too, may relate rhythmically to the speech patterns of a language. For example, words in the Hungarian language are always stressed on the first syllable, and, correspondingly, Hungarian popular melodies (and composed imitations) rarely have an upbeat. In this sort of music, the native-born player may have an advantage in spontaneity and naturalness of delivery.

Without question, the easy availability of recordings in recent decades has begun to affect considerably the stability of such national styles. With the wide diffusion of radios and LP records since World War II, musical culture has become remarkably homogenized. Instead of being principally influenced by the musicians of his native city and country, a young player today is probably quite as familiar with the work of the biggest stars on the international circuit. As a result, national distinctions of instrumental and vocal style are fast breaking down—another reason why older recordings have become an irreplaceable repository of unique performances.

The Changing World of Music

Most of the performers discussed in this book matured before recordings became, for many people, the central feature of musical life. They were formed in a world where virtually all music was "live"—where you could see the people who were making the music and be vividly aware of the human activity it entailed, where every performance was made afresh and a piece came out at least slightly different every time it was played. In that era, too, many amateurs made music themselves and thus had some direct appreciation of what is involved, technically and emotionally, in the study, understanding, and projection of a musical work. The great performer was held in awe, for he could do things that few others—and no machine—could do; every performance was unique and "vanished into air, into thin air" when it was over.

Today, we have at our beck and call an enormous world of music—many times as large as the repertoire that even the most dedicated concertgoer of a century ago could ever have encountered in a lifetime. We can hear—and endlessly repeat—any piece, any performance from that recorded library, without the least physical effort on anyone's part to make the sounds we are hearing. That very availability tends to render commonplace what was surely intended to be—and once was—a uniquely vivid, communicative experience. We cannot go back to that different time, but we can revisit it through historic recordings. The following chapters aspire to bring the reader-listener closer both to the physical aspect of performance and to the intellectual and expressive accomplishments of great instrumentalists, for it is only with active, participatory listening that these recordings are likely to yield their full richness.

NOTE

All recordings cited are monophonic, 33$^1/_3$ RPM LP single disks unless otherwise specified. The country of origin for each cited catalogue number is indicated by the following abbreviations:

US	United States
UK	United Kingdom
F	France
G	Germany

2

KEYBOARDS

Strictly speaking, the piano is really eighty-eight separate musical instruments, each designed to produce a single pitch: a string (or two or three) that will vibrate at a certain frequency, a hammer to set it vibrating, a key and associated mechanism to activate the hammer, and a damper to stop the vibrations when the key is released. Set side by side, these eighty-eight instruments can be controlled by means of a keyboard that brings them within the reach of two hands. There are also foot pedals that can keep the dampers from stopping the vibrations even after the key has been released.

Those eighty-eight notes reach lower than the lowest note of the double bass, and as high as the highest note of the piccolo. With his ten fingers, a pianist can sound a number of notes at once—something that puts within his reach a range of music-making not available to string and wind players, who may be able to sound several notes at once under special conditions, but who are usually restricted to one note at a time, a single line of melody. This means that a pianist can make rich and complex music alone. Other musicians need accompanists, except in special and limited circumstances (for example, a violinist playing the Bach sonatas for solo violin), and this means a counterpull of personality. The pianist presents only himself—and, of course, the music. And he has more space within which to work spontaneously, for he does not have to worry about keeping together with any colleagues.

The directness of that one-man situation, along with the instrument's capabilities of range and polyphony, made the piano the most popular domestic and concert instrument of the 19th century. It could travel to places where orchestras could not afford to go. On it, a skilled player could produce a reasonable approximation of any work in the musical literature, not excluding symphonies and operas. Even today, it remains indispensible in this role during early rehearsals of operas and choral works, although in the home its functions have been largely taken over by the phonograph. And, of course, it is the standard accompanying instrument for voices, strings, and winds in recital.

Piano Tone

To a remarkable degree, piano music depends upon an aural illusion. The piano is really a percussion instrument; the sound is produced by a hammer striking a string. It is a sharp sound, and diminishes quickly after the initial impact. When human voices, violins, and flutes "hold" a note, they continue to generate fresh vibrations, but the piano's "held" note is constantly decaying. The piano isn't a sustaining instrument, merely a resonating one; over the centuries, one of the preoccupations of piano builders was to increase its power of stretching that decaying sound. By releasing the dampers, the pianist can shut off a note before it has died out, but there is no way he can extend it beyond the natural duration of its resonance.

Thus, when we speak of a pianist's "singing tone" we are speaking metaphorically. A singer moving from one note to the next usually connects the two notes, carrying a little sound across the space between them, producing a legato line. The pianist has no way of doing this, but by careful control of the way he strikes the notes and of when he releases them, he can create a very satisfactory illusion of legato.

Piano Technique

Though far from perfect, the piano keyboard is a remarkably efficient device for putting a large number of notes within the command of two hands. The alternation of black and white keys, though it originated historically in the structure of musical scales, is convenient for orientation and also for fingering. The average hand can play five immediately adjacent notes, or stretch out to reach over eight or more white keys. Using the thumb as a pivot (usually on a white key), the four fingers can be passed over it to position the hand over a new group of keys. Much of a pianist's mechanical training is devoted to making such changes of positions rapidly and smoothly: when Horowitz, for example, plays a rippling series of notes from one end of the keyboard to the other, he has not dragged his hand along the keys as fast as possible (this *glissando*, or slide, is a special maneuver only occasionally used), but has actually fingered each note independently, constantly and swiftly repositioning his hand. Nor is that all: he has to get his fingers off the notes as smoothly as he presses them down, or the result will be a smudgy blur rather than a string of pearls.

Such dexterity and coordination are at the heart of the pianist's technique. Remember that the two hands are not identical but opposite in shape, so the same pattern must be fingered differently in each hand. Pianists must master not only the simple scales just described, but also multiple scales. And two scales at once, in thirds or sixths, with the same hand—very much trickier to finger and make smooth. And arpeggios, or broken chords—as it were, scales with gaps in them—requiring much more extended pivoting of the hand. And rapidly repeated notes, which must be carefully gauged so as not to overwhelm the piano mechanism's flexibility. And wide skips, for which the hand must take a flying leap, rather than pivoting and repositioning while still in contact with the keyboard. And the crossing of hands, when one kind of musical activity continues in one place and another skips around above and below it. And trills and tremolos (the rapid alternation of two notes), whereby the piano can fake the sustained tone of other instruments. And so on.

But such feats of speed and dexterity are only part of the complete pianist's technique. Because the pianist can play more than one note at a time, he often finds himself playing both a melody and its accompaniment, or two or more melodies simultaneously. In order to differentiate these different musical threads, the pianist must be able to "bring out" one, playing it louder or more sharply than other notes that he may also be playing with the same hand. Not only a complete independence of the two hands is required, but a complete muscular independence of every finger as well. Rhythmic control is called for, too: a clarinetist may be asked to play a rhythm of three notes to the beat while everyone else plays four, but a pianist sometimes will have to play three with one hand and four with the other—something like the proverbial challenge of patting your head and rubbing your stomach at the same time.

Strength is important, too: the ability to get the maximum tone from the instrument at climaxes. This is a matter of more than mere muscles, for one wants the richest, fullest sound, without letting it degenerate into mere clatter. In such matters, often lumped together under the term "touch," the instrument itself plays an important role; as any professional will tell you, no two pianos are alike. Some are built well and cared for, others are not. Some respond consistently to every variation of touch, others have whims of their own. And of course individual pianos have individual tonal colorings that may make them especially suitable for one or another type of music. Unfortunately for the touring pianist, his instrument is obviously less portable than a tennis racket or a violin, so he is usually at the mercy of the instruments he encounters along the road.

In the concert hall or on television, you may be able to watch the hands of a virtuoso at work, speeding up and down the keyboard or making daring leaps. When you listen to a record, of course, there is no such visual assistance, but with attention and imagination you can visualize what two hands must be going through to produce the sounds you hear—and this adds a fascinating dimension to the listening experience.

VLADIMIR HOROWITZ
Piano

"THE HOROWITZ COLLECTION: CONCERT ENCORES"

Horowitz: Variations on Themes from Bizet's "Carmen" • *Mussorgsky (arr. Horowitz): By the Water* • *J.S. Bach (arr. Busoni): Nun komm', der Heiden Heiland* • *Saint-Saëns (arr. Liszt and Horowitz): Danse macabre* • *Mozart: Piano Sonata in A major, K. 331—Rondo alla turca* • *Prokofiev: Toccata, Op. 11* • *Liszt (arr. Horowitz): Variations on Mendelssohn's Wedding March* • *Mendelssohn: Songs Without Words: Elegie, Op. 85, No. 4; Spring Song, Op. 62, No. 6; The Shepherd's Complaint, Op. 67, No. 5* • *Debussy: Children's Corner—Serenade of the Doll* • *Moszkowski: Étude in A-flat , Op. 72, No. 1; Étincelles, Op. 36, No. 6* • *Sousa (arr. Horowitz): The Stars and Stripes Forever (recorded 1942–51)*

US: **RCA Red Seal ARM1-2717;** *UK*: **RCA VH-020**

The last survivor of an era when keyboard virtuosity was widely pursued for its own sake, Vladimir Horowitz (b. 1904) might well be the most prodigious keyboard technician of all time. A native of Kiev in Russia, he burst upon the Western world in the 1920s and, despite several temporary withdrawals from the concert platform for personal reasons, has retained his special eminence ever since. Married to Wanda, a daughter of the conductor Arturo Toscanini, he has lived in the US since 1940.

Perhaps the best context in which to appreciate Horowitz's remarkable digital powers is this collection of shorter pieces, most of them tailor-made to show off powers such as his. An *étude,* or study, is a piece concentrating on a particular technical difficulty; the example here by Moszkowski features pearly runs that appear first in the right hand (upper part) and then, in the central section, pass into the left hand; notice how Horowitz gives the piece variety by making the left-hand runs more aggressive, less satiny. The same composer's *Étincelles* (Sparks) is an exercise in speed and lightness.

The term *toccata* comes from the Italian verb *toccare* (to touch), and originally referred to a piece that showed off a player's touch at the keyboard. It is now used in a more general sense, as a title for a keyboard display piece. Prokofiev's Toccata begins with repeated notes alternating between the hands. Then, while one hand plays a fast figuration, the other skips back and forth across it, playing two-note patterns. Chords are added, and the patterns grow to fill the keyboard high and low, subsiding once only to build again, the same material driven to an even more clangorous climax. Horowitz's strength here resides not only in his ability to get around all the notes, but also in the almost maniacal steadiness and intensity with which he maintains the momentum and accumulates tension.

Like his fabled predecessors of the 19th century, Horowitz displays many of his most characteristic effects in transcriptions of music originally composed for other media. Ever since the days of Franz Liszt, piano technique has been expanded by the effort to accommodate material idiomatic to other instruments. The slow melodies and florid cadenzas of Italian opera inspired the nocturnes of Chopin, the violin virtuosity of Nicolò Paganini impelled Liszt to imitation on the keyboard, the organ music of Bach was adapted to the resources of the piano.

Busoni's arrangement of Bach's *Nun komm', der Heiden Heiland* (Come, Saviour of the Gentiles) illustrates a typical challenge. In the original, the organist's feet play, on the pedal keyboard, a steady "walking bass"; over it, the hands add two meditative lines; above that, at intervals, comes an ornamented version of the Lutheran chorale melody of the title (the inner voices also draw upon melodic material from this melody). An organist can play the inner voices on one set of pipes, the bass on another, and the melody on a third, thus distinguishing them by tone color alone—and, of course, he has his feet as well as two hands to work with. Ferruccio Busoni, a great pianist and adventurous composer at the turn of the century, managed to fit all this music under just two hands—and, to augment the challenge, he doubled the walking bass in octaves that fully occupy the left hand, leaving the right hand to cope with two inner voices and the melody all at once, three different lines to be distin-

Vladimir Horowitz, perhaps the greatest of modern virtuoso pianists whose rare public concerts have enhanced his legendary status.

guished by subtle shadings of touch and loudness. Horowitz manages this with facility, while playing the piece in a dramatic, somewhat affected style that is surely closer to, say, Rachmaninoff than it is to Bach or Busoni. (For more traditional interpretations, listen to the recordings of Dinu Lipatti and, more recently, Alfred Brendel and Paul Jacobs.)

As often as not, Horowitz makes his own transcriptions, and he often touches up other peoples' to make them more difficult. He gives us, for example, a Mussorgsky song that has been turned into a study in middle-range and bass sonorities, in keeping thick chords clear over a steady slow oscillation in the deep bass. Or a symphonic poem by Saint-Saëns, based on Liszt's transcription: full of feathery arpeggios and alternating loud-soft repeated notes, as well as a dazzling effect near the end where, out of the cloudy resonance hanging over from a fearsome upward run, he salvages the ghostly echo of just a few selected notes. Or a march by John Philip Sousa, in which Horowitz contrives to reproduce with two hands the striding bass, the famous tune in the middle range, and the skirling piccolo obbligato up on top. (The trick here involves dividing the middle-register melody between the two hands; at any given instant, only two things are actually happening, but those two things are constantly shifting among low, middle, and high register so as to give the illusion of constant activity in all three ranges.) The arrangements of the "Chanson bohème" from Bizet's opera *Carmen* and the famous *Wedding March* from Mendelssohn's incidental music for *A Midsummer Night's Dream* are more in the nature of variations than transcriptions: rather than recreating the original work on the piano, their purpose is to adorn it with as many notes as can be fit in, and the original becomes little more than a framework for stunts.

Horowitz's distinctive tone, more metallic than melting, can be memorably sharp-edged when he fires off massive cannonball chords and digs into thundering octaves in his Sousa transcriptions, and he is a master at using the pedal to make such sonorities pile up into great waves. In these recordings from the decade of his greatest activity and technical proficiency, that tone is generally well reproduced, though there is a slight banjoish waver in the earliest track, the 1942 *Danse macabre*. The refinement of his playing is clearly evident in the deceptive simplicities of the Mozart, Mendelssohn, and Debussy selections, though in some of these can be heard touches of the coy mannerism that often makes his handling of the most straightforward melodies maddeningly tortuous. Horowitz's Chopin and Schumann can be intolerably neurotic, and in his playing of longer works articulation of musical structure is often subordinated to his fascination with sonority, texture, and technical display.

Over the years, even during his periods of retirement from concerts, Horowitz has recorded extensively, and the majority of these records are currently available. As suggested, the best of them stem from the 1940s and early 1950s, though his 1930 performance of the Liszt Sonata in B minor remains something of a classic (US: Seraphim 60114; G: EMI/Electrola C-053-00100). A later Liszt collection (US: RCA Red Seal LM-2584; UK: RCA VH-006) includes some dazzling and even appropriate accomplishments, and the 1951 concert recording of Horowitz's own high-handed rewriting of Moussorgsky's *Pictures from an Exhibition* (US: RCA LM-2357; UK: RCA VH-010) is justly celebrated—and not to be confused with his much less exciting studio version of a few years earlier (US: RCA Red Seal ARM1-3263; UK: RCA VH-017). Other specialties include the music of Scriabin (US: RCA Red Seal LM-2005; UK: RCA VH-005), and sonatas by Prokofiev and Samuel Barber (US: RCA Red Seal ARM1-2952; UK: RCA VH-014). Horowitz continues to record today—his technique still remarkable though less consistent, and his mannerisms even more obtrusive.

SERGEI RACHMANINOFF
Piano

"RACHMANINOFF PLAYS CHOPIN"

Chopin: Piano Sonata No. 2 in B-flat minor, Op. 35 • Nocturnes: No. 2 in E-flat major, Op. 9, No. 2 • No. 5 in F-sharp major, Op. 15, No. 2 • Mazurka No. 41 in C-sharp minor, Op. 63, No. 3 • Waltzes: No. 1 in E-flat major, Op. 18 • No. 4 in F major, Op. 34, No. 3 • No. 6 in D-flat major, Op. 64, No. 1 • No. 7 in C-sharp minor, Op. 64, No. 2 • No. 8 in A-flat major, Op. 64, No. 3 • No. 10 in B minor, Op. 69, No. 2 • No. 11 in G-flat major, Op. 70, No. 1 • No. 14 in E minor, Op. posth. (recorded 1920–30)

US: RCA Victrola VIC-1534

To talk about great pianists is, almost inevitably, to talk about the music of Frederic Chopin: a pianists' composer, he wrote nothing that did not use the piano, and precious little that used any other instrument at all. He increased the piano's expressive range and the technical powers of its players. He asked the hands to reach further than before, but his novel figurations always fall naturally under the fingers. He understood the sonority of the instrument, using its resonances to enrich his highly colored harmonies and set off his wide-ranging melodies. Earlier composers based their ornamentation on simple scales and chords, but Chopin devised new, intricate filigrees and arabesques.

Chopin early became a specialty of many pianists, especially those of Polish and Russian birth. Most of these Slavic pianists studied with Franz Liszt, a friend and advocate of Chopin; or with Anton Rubinstein or other Liszt pupils; or with Theodor Leschetizky, a pupil of Liszt's teacher (and Beethoven's student) Carl Czerny. Many of these pianists who made records in the early part of this century—among them Vladimir de Pachmann, Ignace Jan Paderewski, Moriz Rosenthal, Leopold Godowsky, and Ignaz Friedman—don't come across with consistent success. Some of them probably didn't play well in the recording studio, without the accustomed stimulus of an audience; others specialized in a kind of improvisatory, incantatory performance that

Sergei Rachmaninoff, composer and pianist, who played the music of others as brilliantly—and as freely—as he played his own.

doesn't stand up well when abstracted from the concert hall and subjected to repeated examination. Their recordings are fascinating objects of study, and sometimes aesthetically rewarding as well, but they are definitely for the *aficionado* rather than the amateur. At the least, they demonstrate that the so-called authentic Chopin style of the 19th century was no single thing, for each of these Chopinists was a law unto himself. (Good recent reissues of early piano records have come from Desmar in the US, Pearl in the UK.)

One pianist of that generation who does project strongly on records is Sergei Rachmaninoff (1873–1943). Until the Russian Revolution forced him into exile at age forty-five, Rachmaninoff had been primarily a composer and conductor, though he also played his own piano music in public. In need of a surer income in the West, he acquired a repertoire and began a triumphant career as a virtuoso pianist. In his day, Rachmaninoff was regarded as a "modern" player, for unlike those of his contemporaries there was nothing in the least improvisatory about his interpretations; once conceived, they remained essentially fixed (and this may well have something to do with the success of his recordings). Listeners today, however, are likely to be struck first by the "old-fashioned" side of Rachmaninoff's approach to music: he is not above recomposing small details of Chopin's music, or even radically reshaping the dynamics and phrasing of a piece.

The most famous example of this is Rachmaninoff's performance of the Funeral March that is, in its grim way, the most reposeful section of Chopin's feverish, unconventional Piano Sonata in B-flat minor. As Chopin wrote it, the overall dynamic shape of the movement looks like this:

$$p \diagup\!\!\!\!\!\diagup\!\!\!\!\!\diagup \mathit{ff} \diagdown p \quad \mathit{pp} \quad p\diagup\!\!\!\!\!\diagup \mathit{ff} \diagdown p$$

MARCH   TRIO   MARCH (repeated)

The funeral procession approaches and recedes, and then—after the consolatory Trio—approaches and recedes once again. Rachmaninoff, apparently following a tradition established by Anton Rubinstein, shapes it this way:

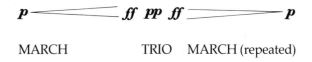

MARCH   TRIO   MARCH (repeated)

Now the procession comes near and departs only once, pausing at its nearest approach for the contrasting message of the Trio. The effect is radically different. Because funeral processions don't pass the same point twice, we understand Chopin's repetition as a formal element, a rounding-off. The Rubinstein-Rachmaninoff view is distinctly more theatrical, more "realistic." It may not be what Chopin wanted, but it is set forth with such authority that, at least temporarily, it wins our assent— and the altered dynamics do make the repetition more interesting.

Chopin ends his sonata with a daring stroke: an uninterrupted stream of rapid, equal notes doubled in both hands—864 of them, before the brief final phrases. This movement could almost be an exercise for the hands to practice playing together—no themes, no articulations, only the barest instructions for dynamics and a tempo marking of Presto. No pianist has ever been content with a completely deadpan run-through, but few have ever elicited from it such a kaleidoscope of glinting colors and wisps of themes as does Rachmaninoff. This is not done capriciously, for it certainly reinforces the underlying structure of the piece, calling our attention to recurring shapes and patterns. A purist might complain that Rachmaninoff has reduced the ambiguity of the piece—but the result is both breathtaking and fascinating.

What Rachmaninoff does in the first two movements of the sonata is less controversial but no less riveting. After the enigmatic slow introduction (which contains the germs of the melodic material of the entire piece), listen to his shading of the accompaniment figure before the pulsing theme begins; in the Scherzo, hear the daring of his attack on the repeated-note themes. Even a half-century later, this remains the most original performance of one of the most original of piano sonatas.

Most of Chopin's works are in short and simple forms. The Waltzes, of which Rachmaninoff recorded a number, are chains of dances, some glittery, some melancholy. In general, the waltz melodies alternate, in ternary (ABA) or rondo (ABACA) patterns; a coda is often added, which may become the emotional climax of the piece, a further and more fevered distillation of ideas that are treated less formally and regularly than before, as if the dancers had suddenly relaxed the constraints of the salon for a brief, intoxicating whirl. Rachmaninoff's clear sense of structure and climax is most effective: the Waltz in E-flat, Op. 18, is entitled "Grand Valse Brillante" by the composer, but the pianist keeps it cool, withholding his ultimate brilliance until the coda.

Some of the recordings of shorter pieces in this Rachmaninoff collection date from the pre-1925 acoustic period, and require a bit of patience with surface noise. Not, fortunately, the Sonata, or the Waltz in C-sharp minor, a performance in which Rachmaninoff at first almost suppresses the dance character, the better to call attention to the intense harmonies; later, in the skirling interlude, the music is ethereally light-footed (in one repetition of this section, the pianist draws out an unsuspected inner voice). On another electrical recording, the Nocturne in E-flat major, Chopin's constantly elaborated melody is stretched and compressed by Rachmaninoff for maximum expressivity. Unlike the distensions of some pianists, which can seem passive and indolent, Rachmaninoff's are tolerable, even hypnotic, because line and momentum, though stretched, never seem to break; he's not toying with the melody, but heightening its character. Arbitrary it may be, but it is also clear and consistent.

Throughout his career as a pianist, Rachmaninoff made records, and he also conducted some of his own music. In 1973, to celebrate his centennial, RCA published a complete edition of all his records, but the only items now in the catalogue are the present Chopin disk and the set devoted to his own piano concertos, which we will discuss later. Nearly every recording Rachmaninoff ever made is riveting; most of them, alas, are of shorter works.

JOSEF LHEVINNE
Piano

"JOSEF LHEVINNE: MASTER OF THE ROMANTIC PIANO"

Chopin: Polonaise No. 6 in A-flat major, Op. 53 • Études: No. 11 in E-flat major, Op. 10, No. 11 • No. 18 in G-sharp minor, Op. 25, No. 6 • No. 22 in B minor, Op. 25, No. 10 • No. 23 in A minor, Op. 25, No. 11 • Preludes: No. 16 in B-flat minor, Op. 28, No. 16 • No. 17 in A-flat major, Op. 28, No. 17 • Schumann: Toccata in C major, Op. 7 • Frühlingsnacht (arr. Liszt) • Debussy (arr. Ravel): Fêtes (with Rosina Lhevinne, pianist) • Johann Strauss, Jr. (arr. Schulz-Evler): Blue Danube Waltz (recorded 1928–36)

US : RCA Victrola VIC-1544

Rachmaninoff's Russian contemporary Josef Lhevinne (1874–1944) came closer to mid-century ideals of musicianship, for the interpretations to be heard on his all-too-few recordings are rarely arbitrary; he approaches the music not as a composer—or re-composer—but as a pianist, filling it to its limits with his prodigious virtuosity. Chopin's Études are ideally suited to Lhevinne's resources, for in each of these pieces a musical work has been built around a technical problem. The Étude in E-flat, Op. 10, No. 11, for example, is composed entirely with extended broken chords—that is, chords that must be "rolled" because they are too wide for the hand to reach all the notes at once. Nor is that all, for within these chords are internal melodies that can be brought out, and the dynamic instructions range from "force" to "sweetness." Not only does Lhevinne roll every chord with perfect evenness, but his complete security means that he shapes the piece on a bigger scale, more fully and richly than most pianists (compare the recording of Alfred Cortot discussed below).

The Étude in G-sharp minor, Op. 25, No. 6, tests the pianist's skill with thirds: scales and trills doubled in the same hand, which call for intricate fingering, superior muscular coordination, and hours of practice. While the right hand spins away at the thirds, the left hand pro-

Josef Lhevinne, a prodigious master of the keyboard but a modest and retiring man, was only too rarely lured into the recording studio.

vides a melodic and harmonic framework. Again, Lhevinne offers an incredible dynamic range and control. His thirds whisper and thunder and cover every possible shading between. One of his specialties was the Étude in B minor, Op. 25, No. 10, with its pounding octaves in both hands; his great colleague Josef Hofmann called it "the most colossal octave playing I have ever heard." The middle section of this Étude may at first seem irrelevant, until the listener realizes that it challenges the pianist to relax and play lyrical octaves, with a melody that derives from the opening sections.

Power, steadiness, security, range, color, musical directness—these are the attributes of Lhevinne's playing; only once in this disk, when he introduces a persistent irregularity into the rhythm of the Prelude in A-flat, does his playing seem mannered and unconvincing. The reverse of the record is as memorable as the Chopin side: notice the suavity of the shading in Liszt's transcription of Schumann's song *Frühlingsnacht,* the verve and tonal palette that he and his wife Rosina unleash in Ravel's two-piano version of Debussy's *Fêtes;* the ease with which he can make his fullest and richest sonority gambol all over the keyboard in Schulz-Evler's ornate and somewhat silly version of the *Blue Danube Waltz.* Although Lhevinne lived in the US from the 1920s on, this one LP contains virtually all of his recordings. Neither the original sound nor the modern transfer is exemplary, and the celebrated beauty of his tone must often be inferred, but at least its depth and variety can be clearly heard. (Rosina Lhevinne outlived her husband by many years, and taught such famous American musicians as Van Cliburn and James Levine before her death in 1976.)

ALFRED CORTOT
Piano

Chopin: 24 Études, Opp. 10 and 25 (recorded 1933–34) • 24 Preludes, Op. 28 (recorded 1933) • Prelude in C-sharp minor, Op. 45 (recorded 1949) • 2 Polish Songs (arr. Liszt; recorded 1939)

UK: **World Records SH-327/8, 2 disks;** *F*: **EMI/Pathé-Marconi/C-153-03090/6, 7 disks (with other Chopin works)**

The French Chopin tradition, unlike the Slavic, stems directly from the composer, who spent much of his life in Paris. The Swiss-born Alfred Cortot (1877–1962) studied with Decombes, one of Chopin's last pupils, and with Louis Diémer. Conductor, teacher, editor, author, collector of a famous library of musical books and manuscripts, Cortot also managed to be one of the great pianists. His technique never reached the heights of Lhevinne's or Rachmaninoff's—and sometimes, through want of practicing, didn't even reach his own best standards—but he made up for it with the power of his musical imagination.

Like the Études, Chopin's Preludes are single-minded pieces, each concentrating on a particular musical or technical idea, but they are smaller in scale—or rather, in length, for some of them (for example, the choralelike pieces in E major and C minor) suggest great edifices in a handful of measures. The twenty-four Preludes of Op. 28 traverse all the major and minor keys, in a sequence that is most effective; Cortot plays them all, in order, and even runs a couple of them together as if to insist on the inevitability of the sequence.

For each piece, Cortot summons a fresh and characteristic sound-image. His rhythmic freedom, greater than Rachmaninoff's or Lhevinne's, is nonetheless firmly rooted in a sense of the music's structure and meaning. The first Prelude, in C major, is a chord progression in which each chord has been shaped into a wavelike fig-

Alfred Cortot became the most famous French pianist of his generation, and was also continually active as conductor, teacher, and editor.

ure, and Cortot's tempo modifications group the waves into phrases; notable, too, is the way in which each wave builds undamped resonance, which is always cleared away so as not to blur the progression from one wave to the next.

In the second Prelude, in A minor, a melody sings over a crabbed rocking accompaniment and arches downward to a new harmonic area. It begins again in a higher key, but this time runs into harmonic ambiguity; Cortot modifies the oratorical arch of the first phrase to a more hesitant diction. With further, still fainter efforts, the melody relapses to a passive stability, and the playing again responds to its sinking fortunes, the initial proud tension ebbing steadily away. Here, as often in his interpretations, Cortot insists on the timbral and sometimes temporal independence of the two elements, melody and accompaniment: in Prelude No. 4, in E minor, the upward-straining melody and the downward-slipping chordal accompaniment lead their own lives metrically, but they always coincide on the downbeats, however freely Cortot may let them diverge between—and each sounds as if played by a different instrument.

This coloristic imagination is perhaps the most distinctive aspect of Cortot's playing. Through dynamic control, careful balancings of chords and lines, he can transform the aspect of a musical figure. The swirling flourishes that decorate the melody of the eighth Prelude, in F-sharp minor, are sometimes smoothly blended, sometimes sharply articulated so that every note makes a rhythmic effect—and the shading between these extremes mirrors the tensions of the harmonies. Similar beauties can be perceived in every Prelude: the flickering melodic fragments coaxed from the web of notes in No. 5, in D major; the charm and grace of the cross-rhythms (three notes in the space normally filled by two beats) in No. 11, in B major; and so on, to the great drama of No. 24, in D minor, with its pounding rhythm in the bass and heroic melodies bursting into runs that sweep up and down the keyboard. (The LP reissue adds Cortot's postwar recording of a separate Prelude in C-sharp minor, Op. 45; like much of his late work, this mixes beautiful details and distressingly uncertain passages.)

A comparison of Cortot's recordings of Études with Lhevinne's will quickly show who has the more magisterial technique. But that would be to miss the point, for in the context of his own playing Cortot's technique and conceptions are perfectly matched, and, despite the occasional scrambly bit, he knows how to make comparable effects. The octave Étude is less monumental than Lhevinne's, but Cortot holds in reserve a sufficient surge of power to generate an equally satisfying conclusion. And much of his playing is technically, as well as musically, ravishing: try the second Étude of Op. 10, in A minor, in which the outer fingers of the right hand must play a continuous legato chromatic scale while the thumb and first finger collaborate with the left hand in staccato chords. In Cortot's hands, that chromatic scale is never static, but swells and fades to give the piece shape and vitality. Indeed, it is easy to hear these performances as sheer music, to forget entirely the technical problems that first inspired them and that must be overcome in their performance.

Cortot made many recordings, though he did not care greatly for the process of "fixing" his interpretations; some of the Chopin pieces he recorded as many as three times. The best versions are collected in the seven-disk French set, which is one of the great monuments of recorded Chopin, especially since the recordings have all been brilliantly and naturally restored by EMI's transfer engineer Anthony C. Griffith. The booklet that accompanies the set, with texts in English and French, includes many interesting quotations from Cortot's writings about Chopin. The two-disk UK set uses the same transfers, but other earlier reissues are from duller and deader tapes prepared in Paris during the 1950s. The only Cortot LP of Chopin regularly listed in the US catalogues is of the Waltzes (Seraphim 60127), from that earlier transfer; it is also one of the less successful performances, with an uncommon number of wrong notes. Still, Cortot's effervescent way with the codas (for example, in Waltzes Nos. 2 and 8) is well worth hearing. (The Griffith transfer of the Waltzes has now appeared separately in the UK: World Records SH-383.) But the big French set, which includes the two Sonatas, the four Ballades, the Barcarolle, and the Fantasie—the core of Chopin's major pieces—as well as the F minor Concerto and various shorter pieces, is very much worth the investment.

Cortot was also a famous Schumann player; the qualities of imagination and fantasy in that music ignited the same spark in him as did Chopin's. Many of his Schumann recordings are collected in a French set (EMI/Pathé-Marconi C-153-03490/2, three disks). *Papillons* can also be found in a recital collection (US: Seraphim 60143), including also works of Chopin, Albéniz, Debussy, and Ravel—a valuable introduction to the scope of his art. But any Cortot recording that might be reissued, even the late ones, is worth a try: for example, his 1947 performance of Chopin's Nocturne No. 16 in E-flat, Op. 55, No. 2 (included in the big French set) is of incomparable intensity and spontaneity, reviving a piece that in most hands seems static and uninspired. Of Cortot's playing of chamber music, more later in this book.

DINU LIPATTI
Piano

Chopin: 14 Waltzes (recorded 1950)
US: CBS Odyssey 32-16-0058, electronic stereo; UK: EMI/HMV HLM-7075

Although born forty years before Dinu Lipatti, Cortot would outlive his pupil by more than a decade. Lipatti (1917–1950) came from a musical family in Bucharest; his godfather was the composer and violinist Georges Enescu, who also figured prominently in the life of Yehudi Menuhin. After escaping from Rumania to Geneva during World War II, Lipatti was stricken with leu-

Dinu Lipatti, in his tragically brief career, played with such mastery of style and technique that his too-few recordings have remained in constant demand.

kemia; despite temporary (and expensive) relief provided by then-newly-discovered cortisone, he died in 1950, only thirty-four years old. Thanks to the efforts of EMI producer Walter Legge, he left behind a significant group of recordings—many of them, including the Chopin Waltzes, made during the final summer of his brief life.

Had Lipatti lived to a full span, he would probably not be in this book at all, for these early recordings would long since have been superseded by stereo and now digital remakes. He belonged to a new generation, the post-Schnabel, post-Toscanini generation to whom respect for the composer's text was an overriding ideal. In Lipatti's hands, the Chopin Waltzes are dances of the utmost elegance and refinement, and the clarity of his playing brings to our attention many beauties of the composer's invention.

Although he breathes comfortably with the music, relaxing to articulate phrases and sections, Lipatti keeps things much steadier than his predecessors, making the desired contrasts of mood and character within the context of a clear dance beat. Of course, these are not waltzes for real dancing, but stylized evocations of the ballroom; still, the maintenance of the illusion has a point, while the rare and purposeful departures achieve a greater expressive effect.

The fourth Waltz, in F major, Op. 34, No. 3, begins with fanfares and then an upward-purling figure that spills into a rapid theme—one which extends over four beats and thus goes out of phase with the three-beat waltz meter (it is fascinating how Rachmaninoff, Cortot, and Lipatti each make us hear a different aspect of this ambiguity). Later comes a theme that begins with a loud downward interval followed by chirruping grace notes; having stated its case, this theme then begins again in an unexpected distant key, and softly. Both Rachmaninoff and Cortot underline this surprise by slowing it down, but Lipatti's continuation of the dancing tempo shows that the contrast of key and loudness is quite enough to make the effect—telegraphing Chopin's punch is hardly necessary. When the first waltz tune returns, it is soon derailed in a novel direction, vanishing into the depths; after a pause, the loud downward theme, now even louder and steeper, brings the waltz to a brilliant close. Again, Lipatti's (and also, in this case, Cortot's) adherence to Chopin's plan is still more effective than Rachmaninoff's slowdown for the "vanishing" passage (fascinatingly mannered though the latter's phrasing of it may be).

The brilliance and clarity of Lipatti's passagework in the faster Waltzes is a continual source of delight. So is his responsiveness to the slightest change of mood: try Waltz No. 10 in B minor, Op. 69, No. 2, with its wistful central section in major that perks up briefly in snappier rhythms, or No. 14 in E minor, Op. posth., a spooky piece with sideslipping harmonies that undermine the dancing right-hand figures. "More objective playing" may be a phrase that suggests duller playing, but Lipatti proves that this need not be so; when he plays an accent or makes a ritard marked in Chopin's score, he does so not mechanically but because he has understood the purpose of the marking and discovered how to integrate it naturally into his conception. (The fake stereo sound of the Odyssey reissue leaves much to be desired, and the UK edition is preferable.)

The bulk of Lipatti's other recordings have recently been gathered in a four-disk package (UK: EMI/HMV RLS-749) and are also available separately (indicated below; the Odyssey editions are inferior). There are Bach and Mozart works from the 1950 sessions, the readings clear and a shade cool (US: CBS Odyssey 32-16-0320, electronic stereo); Chopin's Sonata No. 3 in B minor, Barcarolle, and two shorter works—the Barcarolle an exceptionally ravishing piece of work (US: CBS Odyssey 32-16-0369); and Chopin's Concerto in E minor, from a broadcast with an unidentified orchestra and conductor (US: Seraphim 60007); the Mozart C major Concerto, K. 467, from a concert conducted by Karajan, and Enescu's Third Piano Sonata (US: Angel 35931); two crystalline Scarlatti sonatas, Liszt's *Petrarch Sonnet No. 104,* and Ravel's *Alborado del gracioso,* played with a remarkable combination of grace and Horowitzian brilliance (UK: EMI/HMV HQM-1163). All of these are well worth knowing, as are Lipatti's fresh and direct performances of the Grieg and Schumann piano concertos (US: CBS Odyssey 32-16-0141; UK: EMI/HMV HLM-7046). His final recital, at Besançon in September 1950, was recorded (US: Angel 3556; UK: EMI/HMV RLS-761, two disks); it includes the above-mentioned works by Bach and Mozart, and the Chopin Waltzes, but the studio performances are probably more consistent. A few other concert recordings have turned up, and the hunt for Lipatti tapes continues—but his perfectionism was such that his repertoire increased slowly, and we already have most of the pieces he played. (The only Beethoven sonata he played was the "Waldstein"—and, alas, the BBC tape of that performance was long ago erased.)

ARTUR SCHNABEL
Piano

Beethoven: Piano Sonatas: No. 28 in A major, Op. 101 • No. 29 in B-flat major, Op. 106 ("Hammerklavier") • No. 30 in E major, Op. 109 • No. 31 in A-flat major, Op. 110 • No. 32 in C minor, Op. 111 (Recorded 1932–35)
US: Seraphim IC-6066, three disks; UK: EMI/HMV (forthcoming)

Along with the conductor Arturo Toscanini, the most influential performer of the first half of the 20th century was probably the Austrian pianist Artur Schnabel (1882–1951). Both were advocates of a closer adherence to the composer's written instructions than had previously been the ideal—though they went about realizing this adherence in rather different ways, with rather different results. Schnabel, in particular, expressly allowed a greater role to intuition and to divination of the sense behind the notation than did Toscanini—but in the event both arrived at interpretations that were in significant ways quite as personal and individual as those of less explicitly idealistic performers.

Artur Schnabel, through his many students and his much-admired recordings, is still a vivid and influential presence in the world of music, three decades after his death.

In fact, what we value today about Schnabel's playing of Beethoven, Schubert, Mozart, and Brahms is not its "authenticity"— because it isn't authentic anyway. Schnabel grew up musically in a Vienna dominated by the aged Brahms, and was also a contemporary and friend of Arnold Schoenberg; his music-making strongly reflects that contradictory background. No, what makes Schnabel's playing still powerful and influential is its thoroughness of study, intensity of commitment, profundity of insight—and the vitality and daring with which these qualities are realized at the keyboard. As he grew older, Schnabel concentrated more and more on the central figures of the German repertoire—"music better than it can be performed," he called it. "Unless a piece of music presents a problem to me, a never-ending problem, it doesn't interest me much." In his day, Schnabel's programs were criticized for their unremitting seriousness: "The chief difference between my programs and those of other pianists is that my programs are boring even after the intermission." But the proof of his influence is that today's concert programs are much more like Schnabel's than like Hofmann's or Paderewski's, and do without the flashy *bonnes-bouches* that titillated a sensation-seeking public—and of course that public has changed too.

In important ways, Schnabel's temperament and art were resistant to the idea of recordings. He rejected the idea of a single definitive interpretation—"the very nature of performance is to happen but once, to be absolutely ephemeral and unrepeatable"—and he hated freezing in wax what was only one set of solutions to a complex of interrelated interpretive problems. Furthermore, though Schnabel had a remarkable technique, it was not always dependable, for he would never practice simply for the sake of practicing. Since he would not sacrifice musical truth—what he believed to be the correct tempo or intensity or breadth of phrasing—for the sake of technical security, his recordings have more dropped notes than those of his colleagues (remember that they date from the era before such slips could be easily corrected by tape splicing). One of his reasons for refusing to record for many years might strike us as quaint: "I did not like the idea of having no control over the behaviour of the people who listened to music which I performed—not knowing how they would be dressed, what else they would be doing at the same time, how much they would listen." That is still worth thinking about.

Despite all his reservations, Schnabel finally agreed to make records in the early 1930s, when he was fifty years old, on condition that they comprise all of the Beethoven piano sonatas and concertos—at the time, the most ambitious project of recording ever undertaken. To make it financially feasible, a limited-edition subscription scheme was devised, but the records sold so well that this was dropped after the first two volumes. In fact, the "Beethoven Sonata Society" series went on to include several sets of shorter works and variations as well. First reissued on LP in 1956 and again in every decade since, Schnabel's Beethoven recordings have long since amply rewarded the enterprise of HMV's pioneer producer Fred Gaisberg. And, if Schnabel initially conferred prestige on the phonograph by agreeing to make records, he in turn acquired increased stature and authority from the project, especially in the English-speaking world: he left Germany in1933, moving first to Italy and then to the US and was long one of the most sought-after of teachers (Clifford Curzon, Leon Fleisher, and Claude Frank are among his more eminent students).

All of the Schnabel Beethoven records are worth hearing. I have singled out the set containing the last sonatas, but do not overlook the variations and other shorter works—they contain much treasurable and characteristic playing, especially in the witty, terse Bagatelles. As noted, the sonatas have been transferred to LP several times. The current Seraphim edition, from tapes made in Paris in the 1960s, is uneven: the E major Sonata, Op. 109, sounds thin and quavery, while the C minor Sonata, Op. 111, originally recorded at the same time, emerges firm and pleasant. As of this writing, I have not heard the newest transfers, appearing in Britain in the HMV "Treasury" series. In 1942, Schnabel made new recordings of both Op. 109 and Op. 111 for RCA Victor; for some reason they were not issued until 1976 (US: RCA Victrola AVM1-1410). Quite well recorded, this disk is a valuable supplement to the earlier version—some even consider these performances superior.

Each of Beethoven's final piano sonatas is *sui generis* in form and content. The A major Sonata, Op. 101, begins with a ruminative movement, elliptical in its concision and its avoidance of any clear statement of the tonic (home key) chord, but perfectly clear withal. Instead of a scherzo, there is a brisk and bristly march. The slow movement is more of a transition, leading to—well, first to an unexpected return of the first movement's opening, and then to the true finale, where counterpoint runs rampant, even beyond the explicitly fugal development section.

In this last movement, Schnabel runs into some difficulty, with a scrambly articulation of the principal theme and occasionally manifesting his tendency to rush and blur fast passages when he was ill at ease. Earlier, however, one hears with delight the purposefully exaggerated rhythmic points of the march, the abrupt dynamic contrasts, the lunging *sforzando* (sudden, strong) accents. Characteristic of Schnabel's control of large-scale rhythm is the slow movement, which he treats as one long upbeat to the finale, avoiding all stress accents and confirming the internal points of temporary arrival with slight hesitations or agogic accents. Nor is the final movement a complete loss, for the humor of the coda, with its deceptive resumption of the fugue, is a Schnabel specialty; his perceptive scansion of large-scale rhythms yields a context in which Beethoven's syncopations and other surprises make their most striking effects.

The least successful of the five performances in the late-sonata set is certainly the "Hammerklavier," the Sonata in B-flat major, Op. 106, a casualty of Schnabel's reluctance to make allowances for his technical limitations. (The sonata's nickname has nothing to do with hammers or pounding the keyboard; at the time of the late sonatas, Beethoven was in a very Germanophile mood, and *Hammerklavier* was the German name for the piano. Although he applied it to all the later sonatas, it has stuck to the grandest and most massive of them.) Schnabel takes the first movement very fast at something close to the metronome marking (this is the only piano sonata for which Beethoven provided such markings), and the consequent strain leads not only to some forgivable clinkers but to an unease and tension that contradict the music's authority. Similar problems intrude in the concluding fugue (also taken, bravely, close to the metronome mark), and it is to the perfect rhythmic poise of the Scherzo, the expansive phrasing of the Adagio, and the sheer mastery of keyboard color and pacing in the fantastic, suspenseful transition to the final fugue, that we can best turn our attention. For all its flaws, this recording has many beauties—some of them, ironically, of technical achievement: note the varieties of light and shade that Schnabel can bring to trills, especially the soft trills near the end of the fugue.

Like Op. 101, the remaining three sonatas begin with sonata-form movements of remarkable concision—part of the process whereby Beethoven transfers the center of gravity in the sonata cycle from the first movement, where it lay in the later 18th century, to the finale. But now the common pattern of four movements is set aside in favor of more radical scenarios. In Opp. 109 and 110, this involves terse yet lyrical first movements (as in Op. 101), followed by relatively violent quasi-scherzo movements (that of Op. 109 actually in sonata form, that of Op. 110 in duple rather than the scherzo's proper triple time), and then resolving these contrasts in a final movement of greater range and complexity. In Op. 109, this conclusion is a series of character variations on an elegiac, harmonically static theme; in Op. 110, it is a movement alternating a mournful arioso with a confident fugue that eventually dissolves its increasingly fluid counterpoint into ecstatic melody. Schnabel's performances of both these Sonatas are rich in insights, intense in concentration.

The final Sonata, in C minor, Op. 111, juxtaposes a grim and weighty first movement in minor with a set of variations on a simple cantabile theme in major. Unlike the variations of Op. 109, these maintain a single tempo throughout, with the richness of texture and internal motion steadily increased—a progression interrupted only once, by a variation in which timeless trills appear to replace the steady motion, and vast spaces open between melody and bass (alluding, perhaps, to places in the first movement where the melodic line suddenly plunges from the top to the bottom of the keyboard and back).

This last Sonata may be Schnabel's finest achievement. His uncanny ability to define the inner parts of chordal progressions clarifies the harmonic motion of the slow introduction, and the body of the movement is splendidly articulated within a truly headlong tempo. Note the characteristic Schnabel distortion of the rhythm in the upward twisting turns at the end of the exposition, here expressively apt. The theme of the variations is harmonized with widely spaced chords, but Schnabel makes the notes from different registers of the piano sound perfectly equalized and blended, the melodic line on top always singing out. From this simple beginning, the pianist builds a long arch of song and movement to the richly scored final statement, which floats on a cushion of lower voices in constant but unstressful motion (Schnabel makes it sound easy, but there are very many notes here to be kept under control, with both hands extended to the limits of their capacity). Although Schnabel was accused, by Virgil Thomson among others, of applying a misplaced expressivity to conventional figuration, it is hard to find examples of this in these late sonatas— or perhaps it is more correct to say that Schnabel's demonstration of how little in Beethoven's piano writing is merely conventional, how virtually all of it has an expressive potential, is quite convincing, and has gone on to influence subsequent generations of pianists.

His insistence on examining the purpose of every single note, on discovering the structure and meaning implicit in the notes, his utter rejection of anything casual or unconsidered—this integrity, along with an equivalent commitment to spontaneity in actual performance, constitutes the core of Schnabel's legacy. His solutions to the many problems of Beethoven interpretation are not the only ones—are occasionally, to later ears, unconvincing or exaggerated—but they remain among the most thoughtful and stimulating.

Schnabel's first recordings of the Beethoven Concertos, from the 1930s, have just been rereleased (US: Arabesque 8103-4; UK: World Records SHB-63, four disks), while the 1942 Victor recordings of the Fourth and Fifth Concertos, also worth hearing, were recently deleted. The postwar versions of Concertos 2, 3, 4, and 5, now unavailable, are also good. Aside from Beethoven, Schnabel's most important group of recordings is of Schubert, whose Piano Sonatas owe their present position in the repertoire primarily to Schnabel's advocacy. A complete set of his Schubert recordings, including three sonatas, the Impromptus and Moments Musicals, and various four-hand works (played with his son Karl Ulrich) is promised shortly by Arabesque and World Records. For a good sampling of Schnabel's non-Beethoven repertoire, a recital disk (US: Seraphim 60115) includes a Mozart Sonata and the extraordinary chromatic Rondo in A minor, two Schubert Impromptus, Weber's *Invitation to the Dance*, and three Brahms pieces.

The late recordings of two Mozart Concertos, in D minor, K. 466 and C minor, K. 491, include, in the C minor, Schnabel's own cadenzas, profoundly analytical and wildly unstylish—an interesting insight into the compositional side of his mind (US: Turnabout THS-65046). An earlier and fine Mozart disk couples the Concertos in F major, K. 459 and C major, K. 467 (UK: World Records SH-142). Of Schnabel's many excursions into chamber music, the set of Beethoven Cello Sonatas, with Pierre Fournier, is still available (US: Seraphim IB-6075; G: EMI/Electrola C-147-01382/3), but his collaborations with the Pro Arte Quartet are now hard to find, although the Schubert "Trout" Quintet is available from Germany in a set devoted to classic performances of Schubert (EMI/Electrola C-137-53032/6); reissues of the Schumann and Dvořák quintets are promised by EMI.

WANDA LANDOWSKA
Harpsichord

Bach: *Goldberg Variations, BWV 988 (recorded 1945)*
US: RCA Victrola VIC-1650; G: RCA 26.48017, two disks (with other Bach works)

Only towards the end of the 18th century did the piano became the most commonly used keyboard instrument; but by 1810 it had supplanted the harpsichord nearly everywhere, and the instrument for which Scarlatti, Bach, and Handel had written most of their keyboard music was only gradually revived around the beginning of the 20th century. The single most important figure in that revival was a Polish pianist, Wanda Landowska (1879–1959), who as a girl studied in Warsaw with eminent Chopin specialists but early conceived a passion for the music of Bach. After moving to Paris in 1900, she undertook research into the performance styles of the 17th and 18th centuries, wrote propagandizing articles, and gradually began to introduce the harpsichord into her recitals. In Paris, between the two World Wars, and later in America, where she moved in 1940, Landowska's concerts, recordings, and teaching succeeded in driving away the then-current image of the harpsichord as a thin, tinkly, limited instrument, as well as banishing the idea that most pre-Classical music was primitive and inexpressive.

Instead of being struck by hammers as they are in the piano, the strings of the harpsichord are plucked by quills or leather (today often plastic) plectra. No matter how hard the key is struck, the resulting sound is of the same loudness. To make up for this limitation, instrument makers devised ingenious mechanisms whereby additional strings (at the same pitch, or an octave higher or lower) could be plucked as a result of the same keystroke, thus making sounds louder, more resonant, or different in timbre. In addition, harpsichords with two keyboards, one behind and above the other, were built, in which each keyboard could be attached to different sets of strings (or registers) to permit dynamic and color contrasts. The lute stop, whereby the string is plucked very close to one end, gives a nasal timbre, and there is also a muting device called the buff stop, which presses a strip of leather or felt against the strings at one end and dampens the higher overtones.

In various combinations, these resources furnished the harpsichord with a great variety of sonority—but it was a variety that could not be called into play instantaneously by fingers on the keyboard, as the piano's variety can be. Registers had to be changed mechanically and, except on a few instruments of the later 18th century, required the use of one or both hands. In general, changes of color and dynamics were made between phrases or sections of pieces, and were discrete changes rather than the graduated ones possible on the piano.

Wanda Landowska, though trained as a pianist, became the most vigorous and successsful advocate of the harpsichord, convincing audiences that it was more than a mere antique or toy.

Nor should it be thought that the harpsichord was a standardized instrument like the modern piano (which itself was not standardized on an international basis until the later 19th century). In different times and regions, builders with various tastes and ingenuities came up with individual designs and mechanisms. Today, since scholars have examined and classified the surviving instruments and studied the contemporary documentary evidence, we have a pretty clear idea of which types of instruments were in general use in the regions and periods where each type of music was current, and most modern builders try to reproduce specific types of historic instruments.

This was not always so. In the earlier stages of the harpsichord revival, builders worked from a limited group of old models, some of them atypical or even spurious: the so-called "Bach harpsichord" in Berlin was later proved to have nothing to do with the composer and to have been rebuilt during the 19th century—but by then its disposition of registers had been imitated on a great many instruments built during the first half of the 20th century. The presence of a "16-foot" register (that is, an octave lower than the main strings) on such instruments is particularly problematic historically, for it was in fact very rare in the 18th century.

Early modern builders also took it for granted that some features of modern piano construction would "improve" the harpsichord—for example, the steel frame that permits greater string tension and thus greater brilliance of tone. In fact, it is precisely because the harpsichord's wooden frame did not permit such tension that such brilliant tone is historically inaccurate. Another anachronistic feature was the provision of pedals to make changes of registration, which could thus be made in midstream. And such instruments usually also imitate the size and "feel" of the piano keyboard.

Landowska's favorite Pleyel harpsichords were of this hybrid class, and certain aspects of her playing were clearly conditioned by the unhistorical possibilities they made available. Today, when the emphasis has shifted to the reconstruction and imitation, along historical lines, of authentic instruments, a different range of sonorities, reflecting a more conservative approach to changes of registration, will be heard in recordings of her repertoire. (Curiously, some of the modern works for harpsichord commissioned by Landowska and others are difficult if not impossible to bring off on instruments of authentic 18th-century design, and so there remains a place for the "early 20th-century harpsichord"!

One of Landowska's greatest specialties was Bach's *Goldberg Variations*, possibly the most virtuosic harpsichord work ever composed. This monumental cycle of thirty variations on a sarabandelike "Aria" was published in 1742 as the final installment in Bach's *Clavier-Übung*, a series of exemplary keyboard works. Unlike the sets of variations in Beethoven's late sonatas, the *Goldberg Variations* do not build cumulatively; their sequence is more architectural than expressive—and, indeed, there is little reason to believe that Bach ever imagined the whole cycle would be played complete at one sitting. Be that as it may, modern players and audiences have found it a satisfactory concert piece when played with character and virtuosity.

An encyclopedia of keyboard styles and techniques, the *Goldberg Variations* put special emphasis on the virtuoso possibilities of a harpsichord with two manuals (keyboards). After the first two variations, both introductory, the variations are grouped in threes. The first of each group is a canon (a musical form similar to the round, in which the voices enter one after the other with the same melodic material), and the last is a variation exploiting the double keyboards (which greatly facilitate the playing of two contrapuntal voices in the same register or two voices that constantly cross over each other). Rather than the melody of the "Aria," its bass line is what underlies the variations, much as in the related forms of passacaglia and chaconne (of which Bach also wrote the greatest examples, for organ and solo violin respectively). At the end, the thirtieth variation is a Quodlibet, a form in which various popular tunes are ingeniously combined—in this case, over the persistent bass line of the "Aria." As often in Bach, the choice of material is symbolic: one of the popular tunes goes with the words "I have long been away from you," referring to the long absence of the original melody from its bass—and sure enough, this last variation is followed by a simple restatement of the "Aria," the bass at last reunited with its original melody.

Landowska first recorded the *Goldberg Variations* in France in 1933 (for one of the HMV "Society" issues, like the Schnabel Beethoven series), but she made it again for RCA Victor in 1945—a clearer recording and a tangibly steadier performance. Her tendency to rush a few passages in the earlier version is certainly uncharacteristic, for one of the glories of Landowska's playing is her control of rhythm, her firm stride in both spacious and furious tempos. On an instrument where a dynamic accent (that is, the stress achieved by playing a note louder) is not available, agogic accent (an emphasis achieved by varying the note's length or position in time) becomes an essential resource, but for such accents to make their effect, the surrounding meters must be very regular indeed. (Another kind of accent available on the harpsichord is achieved by ornamentation—a small decoration of a note doesn't make it louder, but it does call attention, which is one reason for the frequent use of ornamentation in keyboard music of the period.) Landowska gives each variation a sure rhythmic profile, and masterfully controls a considerable amount of freedom in the highly expressive Variation 25, in the minor mode.

Bach's theme—and every one of the variations—is in two sections, each marked to be repeated. Landowska's recordings (and most others) omit nearly all these repeats (lest the recording run to two LPs and cost twice as much); the exceptions are a few fast variations, which might seem too brief without the repeats. Curiously, however, Landowska elects in Variations 5, 7, and 18 to repeat the first eight bars after playing the entire variation! The resulting *da capo*, or ABA form, was common enough in the Baroque period—but not in the *Goldberg Variations,* where it does upset an insistent symmetry.

Landowska's instrument, with its resources for elaborate registration changes in mid-stream, as it were, does tempt her into conceiving some of the pieces in terms of dynamic, even orchestral, climaxes that would never have occurred to Bach. It would be foolish, however, to allow any such reservations to deprive us of the virtues of her playing: the sense of architecture, the sheer keyboard virtuosity, and the boundless vitality. (Caution: do not play this, or any other harpsichord recording at a high volume level. Even Landowska's Pleyel produced nothing like the volume of a piano, though it was recorded very closely by RCA.) Some aspects of Landowska's recording remain unsurpassed after thirty-five years, through the listener will find fascinating comparisons with later versions—say, the historically sounder and very musical recording by Gustav Leonhardt (US and UK: Telefunken 6.41198), or the remarkable performance by Glenn Gould on the piano, which he uses in a way that often resembles a harpsichord—very much a "post-Landowska" reading, and an interesting case of reverse influence (US: Columbia M-31820, electronic stereo).

Relatively few of Landowska's recordings are currently available in the US or UK. Some other Bach works, including the Partita No. 2 in C minor, in late and somewhat mannered performances, are coupled with the *Goldberg Variations* in their German edition and available separately in the US (RCA Victrola VIC-1594). Those favorite educational pieces, Bach's Inventions, were her final recording project, and the Three-Part pieces were left unfinished (US: RCA Victrola VIC-1634). Her most ambitious project, in the early 1950s, was a complete recording of *The Well-Tempered Clavier,* full of controversial ideas, almost always fascinating and stimulating (G: RCA 26.35005-EX, five disks).

In Europe before World War II, Landowska made many recordings for EMI, mostly now out of print. The two albums of Scarlatti Sonatas are particularly memorable, and there is a splendid selection of Handel Suites. Throughout her life, Landowska continued to play the piano as well as the harpsichord, and recorded some interesting performances of Mozart in a style that in some respects now strikes us as precious but that is based on much thought and historical knowledge. Concert performances of two Mozart Concertos, as well as the *Concert Champêtre* that Francis Poulenc wrote for Landowska at the harpsichord, have been published; the broadcast sound is variable, the playing invariably stimulating (US: Desmar IPA-106/7, two disks).

EDWIN FISCHER
Piano

Mozart: Piano Concerto No. 22 in E-flat major, K. 482 (with orchestra, conducted by John Barbirolli; recorded 1935) • Piano Concerto No. 25 in C major, K. 503 (with Philharmonia Orchestra, conducted by Josef Krips; recorded 1947).

US: **Turnabout THS-65094**

In the early years of the 20th century, Mozart's piano concertos were rarely played; except for the stormy, proto-Romantic D minor, K. 466, most virtuosos found them insufficiently dramatic for idiosyncratic temperaments. One of the principal advocates of the Mozart concertos—and one of the first pianists to revive the 18th-century custom of leading the orchestra from the keyboard—was the Swiss-born Edwin Fischer. Working in much the same repertoire as Artur Schnabel, Fischer was an equally thoughtful musician, and an even more intuitive and spontaneous player.

Mozart's piano concertos are often singled out as the most inspired realization of the concerto principle, one of the most durable structural ideas in Western music: the encounter, somewhere in the triangle defined by the words competition, confrontation, and contrast, between a small instrumental force and a larger one—most commonly, a single instrument poised against an orchestra. To such an encounter, the two sides bring complementary advantages: the orchestra boasts superior power and greater coloristic variety, the soloist enjoys his virtuosity, his greater flexibility and velocity. Some concertos in the 19th century abandon this central opposition and use the orchestra merely as background and as relief between demonstrations of the soloist's accomplishments. These are not so much concertos as orchestrally accompanied display pieces.

Edwin Fischer, noted interpreter of the solo piano works of Bach, Mozart, Beethoven, and Schubert, was equally at home in chamber music, as accompanist, and as conductor.

The Classical concerto, however, assigns the two sides equal shares. In the first movement, each has its own exposition of thematic material: the orchestra (or *tutti*) first in the home key; then the soloist (who may introduce new themes as well as offering his versions of those first presented by the orchestra), leading to the dominant. After the development, the various themes return in the home key, as is usual in sonata form. Near the end of the movement comes a feature peculiar to the concerto: an apparently definitive cadence in the home key is interrupted and extended by the solo player, who may recall themes from earlier in the movement, modulate into distant keys, combine familiar material in new ways, and generally build suspense until finally the brink of the home key is regained with a trill—and the orchestra reenters to resolve the cadence. This excursion, known as a *cadenza*, was traditionally improvised by the player—who, especially in the 18th century, was frequently also the composer. Some of Mozart's own cadenzas have come down to us in written form, and these are often played today; in the concertos for which no original cadenza survives (including the two that Fischer plays on this recording), modern pianists may select an existing one (Beethoven wrote a famous one for Mozart's D minor Concerto, for example) or prepare their own, as Fischer does.

The slow movements of the Mozart concertos take various forms. In the E-flat Concerto, K. 482, the slow movement comprises a theme and variations, with contrasting episodes between the variations, while that of the C major, K. 503, is in a modified first-movement form with a transition instead of a full development. The finales are usually in rondo form, with solo and tutti alternating in the presentation of themes and episodes. Frequently, as in K. 482, when the principal theme returns there is opportunity for improvised flourishes.

At least a dozen of Mozart's piano concertos are on the highest level, and each of these has its distinctive character, its peculiar formal features. In the present pair, the E-flat Concerto, K. 482 is fluent, elegant, melodic; the C major Concerto, K. 503 is spacious, grand, rather more public in style, and built from more conventional materials (though not conventional in its treatment of them). Even the orchestral color is different: K. 482 uses clarinets, K. 503 the less mellifluous, more pungent oboes. In the first movements, the development section of K. 503 deals at length with a marchlike theme from the exposition, while that of K. 482 is almost entirely texture—harmonies and pianistic figuration, only once pausing to breathe a melody, and that only a distant relative of the second theme from the solo exposition. In K. 482 the emotional weight is in the slow movement, its pathetic theme made more so by the contrasting episodes in major (and by a coda that for a brief moment hints at a happy resolution in major), while in K. 503 the central movement is a point of relative repose between two grander pieces. The last episode of the rondo finale of K. 482 is a spacious minuet, much slower than the main tempo (an idea Mozart had used once before, in another E-flat major Concerto, K. 271).

Recording the E-flat Concerto, K. 482, as early as 1935, Fischer was aware of important matters of performance style that were not widely practiced until after World War II except by 18th-century specialists such as Landowska. In the final movement, he improvises a transition from the preceding cadence to the minuet episode. Earlier, shortly before the return of the principal theme, he fills in with figuration a passage that Mozart notated only with long notes alternately at the top and the bottom of the keyboard—usually a shorthand notation that Mozart used to save time, since he himself would be the soloist (oddly, Fischer does not fill in a comparable passage in the slow movement of K. 503, during the central transitional passage). Similarly, he fills in the harmonies of the minuet episode.

But the spirit of this movement, rather than the textual details, is what makes it remarkable, for Fischer establishes a blithe and dancing character at the very outset and confirms it with each episode. After his cadenza, with its ingenious combination of the main rondo theme and the minuet, he plays with the upbeat to the theme and brings it gradually back to tempo, an effect at once touching and delightful. His final statement is decorated with impudent but perfectly apt improvised scales, and Mozart's joke ending (which briefly pretends that we will now have the second theme once again) is charmingly handled.

The anonymous orchestra of 1935 is not up to Fischer's level, and its tentative playing occasionally distracts from his work in the earlier movements. In the passagework of the first movement's development, Fischer fluently shapes the runs up and down the keyboard; by accent and shading he gives them a sense of destination, a flux of tension to match the harmonic ebb and flow. The slow movement theme is rather desultorily played by the strings, but Fischer then shapes it much more firmly, and the winds play their interludes with some skill. The first-movement cadenza uses a richer harmonic language than Mozart's concerto, but it unfolds one radiant surprise of a modulation, and the ending is ingenious—Mozart seen through Brahmsian eyes, perhaps, but seen with affection and understanding.

The postwar recording of the C major Concerto boasts fuller sound, a more distinguished orchestra, and the same mastery of shape: note how, at the piano's first entry, Fischer avoids any definitive confirmation of a downbeat until the orchestra reenters with the grand opening chords. The slow movement is limpidly played, and there is much rhythmic sport in the finale; in the preparation for the return of the second subject, Fischer makes a startling, impish rhythmic shift. This recording, the first postwar version of the C major Concerto, played an important part in establishing the piece in the repertoire; less obviously appealing than other, more melodic concertos, this one needs a performance of breadth and weight to make its points.

Fischer recorded other Mozart concertos before the war—in general, his best period technically. His favorite collaborator among conductors was Wilhelm Furtwängler, whose death in 1954, along with Fischer's own paralytic condition, darkened the last years of the pianist's life. Fischer and Furtwängler made only one studio recording, of Beethoven's "Emperor" Concerto— a performance at once impetuous and grandly rhetorical (US: Turnabout THS-65072; G: EMI/Electrola C-027-00803). Even more wonderful is a wartime performance recording of Brahms's Piano Concerto No. 2, in which the give-and-take of solo and orchestra is remarkably free and easy; the piece is sometimes too much for Fischer's technique, but the grandeur of his spirit comes through nonetheless (G: EMI/Electrola C-149-53420/6, a seven disk set devoted to Furtwängler conducting Brahms orchestral works, including splendid performances of the Second, Third, and Fourth Symphonies).

Among Fischer's solo recordings, there are Beethoven Sonatas (G: EMI/Electrola C-147-01674/5, two disks, contains five sonatas, including the "Pathétique," "Appassionata," Op. 110, and Op. 111), the Schubert Impromptus (UK: World Records SH-195; a wonderful performance of the "Wanderer" Fantasie is currently unavailable), and a number of Bach works, including a complete version of *The Well-Tempered Clavier*—another of HMV's "Society" publications, full of thought and insight (scheduled for reissue by EMI).

Fischer greatly enjoyed playing chamber music, especially in a trio he formed with the German violinist Georg Kulenkampff and the Italian cellist Enrico Mainardi, but they never made recordings; later, after Kulenkampff's death, the Viennese violinist Wolfgang Schneiderhan joined the trio, and several of their broadcast concerts have found their way into disks (US: Discocorp BWS-735, two disks of Beethoven, Mozart, and Schumann, and BWS-739, containing two Brahms trios; the Beethoven "Archduke" is also available in Europe as Cetra LO-518). Fischer's playing of the opening of the slow movement of the "Archduke," seemingly so simple yet with the chords impeccably balanced, the phrases masterfully shaped, is a perfect example of the directness and profundity of his playing, but these concert performances are very inconsistent. Another notable collaboration is a recital of Schubert songs in which Fischer accompanies Elisabeth Schwarzkopf (US: Angel 35022; UK EMI/HMV ALP-4843).

Aside from the concerto accompaniments that he conducted from the keyboard (including postwar versions of Beethoven's Third and Fourth Concertos, unevenly played by Fischer the soloist yet very grandly directed), Fischer led a fine prewar version of Haydn's Symphony No. 104, and several other works, all long and regrettably unavailable. Most Fischer recordings are worth hearing, and only a few of the postwar series disappoint. Less explicitly intellectual a musician than Schnabel, his playing is often more direct; his mastery of delicate tonal shadings attests to a technical control that is in no way diminished by his evident deficiencies in other realms. Fischer's playing rarely calls attention to itself, and most of the time is neverthless both individual and convincingly right in diction and logic.

SOLOMON
Piano

Brahms: Piano Concerto No. 2 in B-flat major, Op. 83 (with the Philharmonia Orchestra, conducted by Issay Dobrowen; recorded 1947)

US: Turnabout THS-65071; *UK:* EMI/HMV SLS-5094, four disks (with other concertos)

Known as a child prodigy simply by his first name, the English pianist Solomon (b. 1902) retained that designation throughout a distinguished career that ended prematurely in 1956 when a paraplegic stroke brought about his retirement from the concert stage. Solomon studied with Mathilde Verne, a pupil of Clara Schumann, and later with the French pianist Lazare Lévy, the noted organist Marcel Dupré, and with Dr. Rumschisky, a Leschetizky pupil. With this eclectic background, he matured from the boy wonder who had made his debut at eight playing the Tchaikovsky First Piano Concerto into that rarity, a modest, unostentatious, but commanding virtuoso.

That combination is heard at its most effective in Brahms's Second Piano Concerto. Brahms was himself a pianist of remarkable powers: in her diary, Clara Schumann described him playing his own music, with "his beautiful hands which overcame the greatest difficulties with perfect ease (his things are very difficult)." In his concertos, Brahms takes up where Beethoven had left off in the "Emperor" Concerto, presenting the solo instrument as competitive with the orchestra in power as well

Solomon, the English pianist whose career was interrupted in 1956, is still much admired through his recordings, which combine technique and musical probity in equal measure.

as in finesse. (By Brahms's day, of course, the piano had developed into a louder, more resilient instrument; one can't help wondering how Beethoven's wooden-frame instruments withstood the climaxes of the "Emperor Concerto"!)

Brahms follows Beethoven's lead by introducing the piano at the beginning of his concerto; at first in quiet dialogue with the horn and then in a formidable cadenza-like passage, the solo instrument establishes its range and power, and, in a striking reversal of roles, builds up the tension for the first big orchestral entry (in the Classical concerto, of course, it is the orchestra that prepares for the soloist). Thereafter in his first movement, Brahms maintains the basic outlines of Classical first-movement form with double exposition, but there is no concluding cadenza. (Beethoven, in the "Emperor Concerto," had already decided not to leave such an important matter as the cadenza to the soloist's discretion, and wrote it out; presumably he could see that concertos were more and more often being played by someone other than the composer, and he grew increasingly reluctant to leave the working out of a substantial, and crucially placed, portion of his work in the hands of a stranger.)

Brahms's first movement is big in several senses: power, time scale, breadth of gesture. And it is followed by an unusual movement, a stormy Scherzo that increases the work's range of contrast beyond that usually found in a concerto—customarily in three movements, fast-slow-fast. Yet large parts of these first two movements are carried on at less than full voice, while trumpets and drums absent themselves entirely for the final two movements. The generally inward slow movement leads to a restrainedly cheerful finale in Brahms's best Hungarian gypsy style—a conclusion lighter in manner and distinctly less ostentatious than the final curtains of the concertos most beloved by thundering virtuosos.

The remarkable aspect of Solomon's performance is his complete command of all aspects of this concerto. He has the accuracy and strength and reach (Brahms must have had huge hands!) to rise to every demand of the first movement without ever showing signs of strain, and the sensitivity to color and shape the wondrous rustling piano figurations under which the recapitulation creeps in almost unobserved, on the heels of a subtle harmonic side-slip. The Scherzo never becomes ponderous, though the cross-accents in the bass at the beginning are forcibly stated (throughout, the orchestral work under the Russian-born conductor Issay Dobrowen is admirable), and powerfully restated by the pianist when they return later in the movement. Notice, too, during the major-key Trio, after a sudden pause, how the pianist takes off with *sotto voce* double octaves—in Solomon's hands, like a distant but intense flash of lightning.

The beautiful theme of the slow movement expounds a metrical ambiguity: are the six beats of its bar made up of three groups of two (as in the solo cello's melody), or two groups of three (as in the pizzicato lower strings)? As the music progresses, various possibilities are explored, and this performance sets them all forth clearly without foreclosing any. Later, when the more vigorous contrasting section seems to be subsiding to the calm of the piano's first entrance, a deep and distant chord propounds a new direction: two clarinets spin, *dolcissimo* (very sweetly) over quiet piano arpeggios, a long-drawn-out melody subtly highlighted by gleaming piano notes. This breathtaking passage could not be more raptly played; time seems to be standing still when the cello melody finally returns (although not, until after a further shift, in the home key).

Brahms marked his finale Allegretto grazioso, and this performance is one of the rare ones that really fulfill the "gracious" part of that instruction. Solomon is downright sportive, as well as maintaining the transparency of texture characteristic of all his playing.

The other Romantic concertos in the HMV set that contains the Brahms Second Concerto are comparably successful (and also available separately in the US): the Brahms First Concerto (US: Turnabout THS-65110), the concertos of Grieg and Schumann (US: Quintessence PMC-7055), and Tchaikovsky's First Concerto and Liszt's Hungarian Fantasia (US: Turnabout THS-65108). Many of Solomon's recordings are currently available, but not, unfortunately, his impressive Chopin disks nor his powerful performance of Brahms's Variations and Fugue on a Theme of Handel. His debilitating stroke interrupted the recording of a Beethoven Sonata cycle; the eighteen Sonatas that he finished have been reissued as a boxed set in the UK (EMI/HMV RLS-722, seven disks) and in partial, scattered form in the US: Sonatas 8, 14, and 23 on a single disk (Seraphim 60286), Nos. 21 and 28/32 in a box (Turnabout THS-65068/70, three disks), and two others as fillers to Beethoven Concertos (No. 26 on Seraphim 60308; No. 27 on Seraphim S-60016). Although never less than admirable, played with musical integrity and seriousness of purpose, these performances are on the muted, impersonal side, with a limited range of tonal color. Many passages are illuminated by Solomon's musical honesty and superb technique, but one rarely encounters the temperament, the daring, the revelatory flashes that make the performances of Schnabel and Fischer so endlessly fascinating. For a sample, you might try Solomon's reading of the last Sonata, Op. 111, more personal and forceful than most of his work.

The same limitations apply to his playing of the Beethoven Concertos, which, moreover, do not enjoy the magisterial level of accompaniment that Furtwängler (and Fischer himself) provided for Fischer. These are available as a box in the UK (EMI/HMV SLS-5026, four disks) and as singles in the US, one concerto to a disk (Seraphim S-60016, 60308, S-60019, 60309, and 60298). His work on a group of recordings of Mozart—three Concertos, K. 450, K. 488, and K. 491, and two Sonatas, K. 331 and K. 576—is also somewhat reserved (UK: EMI/HMV RLS-726, two disks). In the field of chamber music, Solomon's superb playing is not quite matched by his string colleagues in a 1943 recording of Beethoven's "Archduke" Trio (US: Arabesque 8032), and Piatigorsky's playing in the same composer's Cello Sonatas lacks the intellectual distinction of Solomon's work at the piano (UK: EMI/HMV RLS-731, two disks).

SERGEI RACHMANINOFF
Piano

Rachmaninoff: Piano Concertos: No. 1 in F-sharp minor, Op. 1 (with the Philadelphia Orchestra, conducted by Eugene Ormandy; recorded 1939–40) • No. 2 in C minor, Op. 18 (with the Philadelphia Orchestra, conducted by Leopold Stokowski; recorded 1929) • No. 3 in D minor, Op. 30 (with the Philadelphia Orchestra, conducted by Eugene Ormandy; recorded 1939–40) • No. 4 in G major, Op. 40 (with the Philadelphia Orchestra, conducted by Eugene Ormandy; recorded 1941) • Rhapsody on a Theme of Paganini, Op. 43 (with the Philadelphia Orchestra, conducted by Leopold Stokowski; recorded 1934).

US: RCA Red Seal ARM3-0296; *UK*: RCA AVM3-0296, three disks

Of Sergei Rachmaninoff's five scores for piano and orchestra, three soon established themselves as standard works: the Second and Third Concertos and the *Rhapsody on a Theme of Paganini*. The composer chafed under this public preference (though he resented still more the ceaseless demand for his Prelude in C-sharp minor, a piece that he came to speak of simply as "It"), but it is well founded. Though the First Concerto was revised some years after the Third was composed, its invention is clearly of a lesser order, while derivative thematic material and fragmentary structure clearly assign the Fourth Concerto to the bottom of the ladder.

By the end of the 19th century, the Classical concerto form had withered away. As early as Mendelssohn, the double exposition of themes, once by orchestra and once by soloist, had been virtually abandoned in favor of a single one shared by soloist and orchestra, thus reducing the explicitness and formal inevitability of their opposition. (That Brahms, in his concertos, still favored the double exposition is a manifestation of his fascination with his Classical forbears.) Often enough, the Romantic concerto became little more than a showcase for the soloist, with the orchestra functioning more as a frame for a picture than as an equal participant in a significant dialogue.

Such concertos tended to be discursive rather than closely argued—episodic, with the tension and expectation generated principally by the soloist's feats of virtuosity. Rachmaninoff's concertos, although they assign a more than respectable role to the orchestra, nevertheless inhabit the same formal limbo; attractive as the succes-

*Eugene Ormandy, conductor of the Philadelphia Orchestra,
with Sergei Rachmaninoff, who admired the Philadelphia above all
orchestras; with it, he recorded all of his piano concertos.*

sive sections are, they do not always follow with the
logic, the necessity, of the materials of a Mozart or
Beethoven concerto. Symptomatic is the fact that in the
Third Concerto, even the composer found it desirable to
make some cuts, to tighten the piece up—and this even
though the Third Concerto is thematically the most integrated of the four, with virtually all its themes derived
from the melody that opens the first movement. Rachmaninoff makes four cuts in his recording (one each in
the first two movements, two in the third), and it has
been established that he customarily made at least three
of them in concert performances during his later years—
proving that they were not made simply to fit the music
into the straitjacket of 78 RPM record sides. The first of the
cuts in the third movement entirely removes the intital
presentation of the lyrical second theme, which thus sur-
faces only briefly and enigmatically near the end of the
piece, at a point when new thematic material is distinctly
out of place.

For some time, other pianists followed Rachmaninoff's lead, and even made further cuts, but more
recently the tendency has been to play the piece complete. Vladimir Horowitz, who studied the Third Concerto with Rachmaninoff and whose interpretation won
the composer's approval, has progressed, in his three recordings, from four cuts to none at all (his 1930 recording
is on US: Seraphim 60063 and G: EMI/Electrola C-053-

03038; the 1951 version on US: RCA Red Seal CRM4-0914, four disks, with other concertos, and UK: RCA VH-004; the 1978 concert recording on US and UK: RCA CRL1-2633). Rachmaninoff wrote two cadenzas for the first movement of this concerto, though he stated his preference for the lighter, shorter one so strongly that one wonders why he allowed the other one to be published at all. Here, too, there has been a trend in recent years away from the composer's preference; pianists such as Van Cliburn, Lazar Berman, and Vladimir Ashkenazy have preferred the more massive alternate (Horowitz has stuck to the shorter one).

Clearly, then, the precedents set by Rachmaninoff's own recording are not considered to be binding by his successors. Interestingly, the pianists who opt for the more massive cadenza tend to favor a more massive and stately approach to the entire first movement: Cliburn's performance (currently unavailable from RCA) is exceptionally convincing in this respect, reminding us that the ultimate criterion is not necessarily what you do, but how you do it.

For that matter, hardly anybody has tried to emulate Rachmaninoff's exceptionally fleet and volatile approach to this movement; even in his first recording, Horowitz did not risk such a tempo—but the composer brings it off. The purling grace of the circling and climbing first theme, the feline lunge of the scherzando motive that prefigures the second theme, the direct and unfussy phrasing of that second theme (and the authoritative flexibility of the tempo), the power of the climaxes are all very special and characteristic of Rachmaninoff's playing. (He is, in fact, at least as free with his own music as with Chopin's!) In the middle of the slow movement comes an episode in which the soloist describes a rapid filigree theme over a fast waltz bass; as usual, Rachmaninoff makes his passagework glisten with life and color. This type of writing—sometimes as an inner voice under a slower-moving melody, often marked scherzando or leggiero—is prominent throughout all the concertos, and, as played by the composer, never fails to fall freshly upon the ears.

To catalogue all the beauties of the playing in these records would require a book all to itself. But one should not overlook, through fascination with individual details, the consistent intensity and concentration in Rachmaninoff's playing. This is most evident, certainly, in the

Paganini Rhapsody, where the economical structure—twenty-four variations on the acerbic theme and a coda—can become episodic if not given overall shape and tension. (Although not the latest among these recordings, this is one of the best-sounding; unfortunately, the microphone arrangements for the Ormandy sessions in 1939–41 present the piano with rather less clarity.) Equally notable is the absence of any vulgarity in the playing, of any sensationalizing of the virtuosic writing for the sake of effect (a tendency not avoided in any of Horowitz's recordings of the Concerto, for example).

Rachmaninoff also conducted, and he made for RCA several recordings of his own music with the Philadelphia Orchestra—all, alas, currently unavailable, but well worth searching for: the Third Symphony, the tone poem *The Isle of the Dead* (slightly cut, but a hypnotically intent performance), an orchestral version of the *Vocalise*. And his playing of his many short solo piano pieces should be snapped up whenever reissued.

SERGE PROKOFIEV
Piano

Prokofiev: Piano Concerto No. 3, in C major (with London Symphony Orchestra, conducted by Piero Coppola; recorded 1932) • Diabolical Suggestion. Op. 4, No. 4 • Fugitive Visions, Op. 22—Nos. 3, 5, 6, 9, 10, 11, 16, 18 • Gavotte from Symphony No. 1 ("Classical") • Andante from Piano Sonata No. 4 in C minor, Op. 29 • Tales of the Old Grandmother, Op. 31—Nos. 2, 3 • Gavotte, Op. 32, No.3 • Étude, Op. 52, No. 3 • Landscape, Op. 59, No. 2 • Pastoral Sonatina, Op. 59, No. 3 (recorded 1935)

G: EMI/Electrola C-053-03037; UK: World Records SH-209 (Concerto only, with Ravel: Piano Concerto in G, played by Marguerite Long, conducted by Ravel)

Like Rachmaninoff, Serge Prokofiev (1891–1953) chose to live in the West after the Bolshevik Revolution; unlike his older colleague, however, Prokofiev returned home in 1936, after several exploratory tours. His music was much more difficult for audiences to grasp than Rachmaninoff's—more so than the difference of less than twenty years in their ages would suggest, for Rachmaninoff began as a conservative composer and did not alter his style very much over his whole career. Although Prokofiev played the music of other composers as well as

Serge Prokofiev, sketched by the Russian Ballet designer Natalia Gontcharova, during the years when, as pianist, he was the most brilliant and persuasive advocate of his own music.

his own, he was hardly a candidate for mass popularity as a pianist, and he must have hoped that Soviet Russia would provide more opportunities, especially for his difficult and mostly unperformed operas (it didn't work out that way, but that is another story).

Before he left Western Europe, Prokofiev recorded his most popular piano concerto and a selection of shorter works for solo piano. At the time, making these records was a daring venture on the part of French HMV, for even in small doses modern music did not sell well. That they exist at all is probably due to the impetus of Piero Coppola, the Italian-born conductor who directed the French branch of His Master's Voice and who was a friend and supporter of Prokofiev. There are too few souvenirs of his playing; because of the war and ill health, Prokofiev made few public appearances in later life, and little seems to have survived of his playing on Soviet disks, although there are a few examples of him conducting—which he did rather less magisterially. But these Paris-made disks are irrefutable evidence of his keyboard powers.

The most characteristic aspect of Prokofiev's piano writing is the relentless, mechanistically regular flow of notes or chords, such as we have already heard in Horowitz's recording of the Toccata, Op. 11. The piano as a percussion instrument and the performance as a feat of endurance—these are the most immediately striking features of such works as the *Diabolical Suggestion,* which Prokofiev first played in public in 1908, at the age of seventeen. And despite the expansively Romantic introductory melody of the Third Piano Concerto, it is a piece dominated by almost ceaseless activity from the piano soloist, most of it in toccatalike virtuoso work. In fact, the piano is active for approximately seven-eighths of the Concerto's duration, nearly all of it technically strenuous writing. Prokofiev was a master of this kind of playing; he never flags, and he never sentimentalizes: the marchlike second subject of the first movement, more melodic than the busily running first subject or the crashing-up-and-down chords that follow, is not relaxed in any way, nor is there any soupiness about the development of that Romantic-sounding opening melody. (Prokofiev's first movement is in a greatly simplified form, the exposition followed by a section that brings forth all the same material in sequence but now in a more extended version—a combined development and recapitulation.) The principal material of the third-movement rondo calls for similar skills.

Many pianists have learned to match Prokofiev's mechanical prowess. In fact, the most personal aspects of his playing are found elsewhere. The second contrasting episode of the Concerto's third movement presents an expansive melody, somewhat drily scored for winds; its incipient lyricism is at first contradicated by a sassy marchlike tune from the piano, primarily emphasizing repeated notes. This latter is usually played very straight and even, but Prokofiev gives it a variety of shading that suggests something more pensive, a more apt preparation for the surprisingly lush development of the expansive melody that now ensues.

At the beginning of the Concerto, in the strings' phrasing of the introductory melody, you will notice a degree of *portamento* (sliding from note to note) that seems, in general, alien to the brash style of this piece, though quite in place when the Philadelphia Orchestra does similar things with Rachmaninoff's lusher themes. Remember that Prokofiev's Concerto was only eleven years old at the time of this recording, and, although the composer may have mastered his own style, orchestras were still more accustomed to older styles. In the third variation of the slow movement, in which the piano's strong beats are supposed to be out of phase with the orchestra's, Prokofiev himself does not succeed in making this nearly as clear as more recent pianists do—a case where even the composer has not fully realized the implications of his own writing.

The collection of solo pieces is equally fascinating. The *Diabolical Suggestion* is of a steely intensity that would not disgrace Horowitz. One can admire, too, the way Prokofiev keeps the low-bass textures clear in the Andante from his Fourth Piano Sonata, his natural shaping of the irregular phrase-lengths of the *Landscape* (a piece only two years old at the time of the recording). The most vivid playing is in the brief, mostly acerbic character pieces entitled *Fugitive Visions*. The mercurial, scampery playing of Nos. 5, 6, 10 and 11 is very personal, often distorting the meter for humorous effect. In No. 17, Prokofiev makes the triple-meter melody drag marginally against the flickering duple-meter pattern of the other hand, putting an expressive point on what might otherwise have remained a merely mechanical cross-rhythm. The melancholy waltz that is No. 18 does not lag into sentimentality. (A fascinating exercise is comparison of Prokofiev's performances of these pieces with those of more recent Russian virtuosos, including the deadpan Gilels and the moody Richter; even in such aphoristic music, the difference can be as between night and day.)

3

WINDS AND BRASS

Broadly speaking, a wind instrument produces sounds by setting in vibration a column of air, the length of which determines the pitch of the sound: a longer air column produces a lower pitch. The two principal subclasses of wind instruments are traditionally known as woodwinds and brass, but this nomenclature is not entirely accurate; some windwinds, notably the flute, are now usually made of metal.

A more significant distinction is based on the way the air column is made to vibrate. In the brass instruments—the horn, trumpet, trombone, tuba, and their relatives—the player's lips are pressed against a cuplike mouthpiece and put into motion by his breath; the motion of the lips makes the air column within the tubing of the instrument vibrate. In the flute, the lips aim the stream of breath at the far edge of the breathhole, and that edge breaks the stream into vibrating waves that are transmitted to the air column inside the instrument. In a third type of tone production, the player's lips and breath set in motion a mouthpiece of reed that moves the air column inside the instrument (in the clarinet, a single reed set against the player's lower lip; in the oboe and bassoon, a double reed held between the lips).

Playing Techniques

Each of these methods of tone production has its peculiarities, and each produces a distinctive sound. All demand exceptional control of the player's *embouchure* (mouth shape), of his lips, which are, in a real sense, part of the instrument. So, too, is the player's tongue, which is used to release and impede the flow of his breath; the syllable *tu* (or, in the brass, the harder *du*) is used to start the tone, to give it a strong kick that will overcome the inertia of the mouthpiece and the air column. In fast music, much agility is demanded of the tongue as well as of the lips and fingers. Because of this physical participation in the production of the sound itself, the tone of wind and brass instruments can be a particularly personal matter. (In the double-reed instruments the player himself traditionally cuts and shapes his own reeds from pieces of cane, because the reed's contours, flexibility, and other characteristics must be so finely adjusted.)

Without modifications, the air column within a tube of a given length will produce only a single pitch—hardly enough to qualify it as a musical instrument. (The organ is really many separate wind instruments, each producing a single pitch and controlled from a keyboard.) Over the centuries, several methods have been devised for producing additional pitches from a single pipe. The player's lips can be trained to isolate the overtones of the fundamental pitch, the notes that vibrate at a half, a third, a fourth, and smaller partials of the tube's length— a technique basic to brass instruments (some of which, such as the bugle, produce all their notes this way). To fill the gaps in this overtone series, valves that connect additional lengths of tubing (or, in the trombone, the slide that lengths the basic tube), lower the pitch of the fundamental and its overtones; valves were first added to the brass during the 19th century.

In woodwind instruments, holes bored in the tube and covered by the fingers can be opened, shortening the effective length of the air column and raising the pitch. In addition, mechanical keys can be added to control holes that would normally be too far apart for the fingers to reach (especially important in the lower-pitched instruments with longer tubes, such as the bassoon and contrabassoon). And the fundamental scale thus generated can be extended to higher octaves by "overblowing"—that is, by isolating partials, as in the brass instruments, although only the lower partials are used in the woodwinds.

Tonal Characteristics

Naturally, the particular construction, tone production, and historical development of each of the wind and brass instruments has produced specific strengths and weaknesses for composers to exploit or to avoid, for players to master or conceal. The clarinetist, for example, has to equalize the notes between his rich (*chalumeau*) lower register and his much brighter (*clarino*) register above, so that in scales this register break is not obtrusive to the listener. But a composer may also take advantage of such a register difference: a classic case in point is the Trio of the Minuet in Mozart's Symphony in E-flat major, K. 543, where one clarinet playing a melody in the clarino register is accompanied by another gurgling away in the chalumeau.

For another example, the modern metal flute tends to a hollowness of tone in its lower notes that was not characteristic of the older instruments, although in compensation it offers greater brilliance and security in the uppermost notes. Thus, players performing older flute music on the modern instrument have to exercise special care, since it was written for—in effect—a different instrument.

Playing a wind instrument is a matter of coordinating breath, tongue, lips, and fingers in complex combinations. Although the holes and valves of the instrument are physically fixed, the pitches they produce are not as inflexible as those of the piano, and need to be constantly adjusted by the player's lips to be precisely in tune. An air column has its own inertia; once vibrating at a particular pitch, it may resist attempts to change its length, and the player has to develop a feeling for how quickly he can make it change. Miscalculation will result in unexpected and decidedly unwelcome noises—squeaks, squeals, or intrusive intermediate notes. In the hands of master players, the instrument's inequalities and compromises should of course, be concealed; we should hear only music, its lines and colors.

Wind Soloists

Though the repertoire for solo wind instruments is extensive, few works aspire to the stature of the great piano and string literature. This may in part be a function of the very distinctive character of the instruments, which makes them less adaptable to the protean roles that the more neutral strings and the more versatile piano have been assigned. Without such major works, the demand for solo wind players has been limited, and until recently few players found it feasible to leave the economic security of an orchestral position to pursue careers as full-time soloists. For a long time, the wind players best known on records were those who worked in orchestras in the major recording centers (especially London) and were thus readily available when wind repertoire was to be recorded. That is the principal reason why the players discussed in the following section are all Europeans, for during the prewar years very little nonstandard repertoire was recorded in the US. (One other famous British wind player of the period, the clarinetist Reginald Kell, would be here as well, but his only recording currently in circulation, the Brahms Clarinet Quintet, is part of a seven-disk set, described in the chapter on the Busch Quartet.) Today, of course, the portability of tape recorders has made it possible for players anywhere in the world to be recorded.

MARCEL MOŸSE
Flute

Bach: Suite No. 2 in B minor for Flute and Strings, BWV 1067 (with the Adolf Busch Chamber Players; recorded 1936) • *Brandenburg Concerto No. 5 in D major, BWV 1050 (with Adolf Busch, violin; Rudolf Serkin, piano; Adolf Busch Chamber Orchestra; recorded 1935)*

US: Seraphim 60357; *UK*: World Records SHB-68, two disks (Suite only, with Suites 1, 3, 4)

Marcel Moÿse (b. 1889) was the leading French flutist of the first half of the 20th century; he played with the major Paris orchestras, and taught at the Paris Conservatory. As a soloist, Moÿse introduced many important French works, and he was a member of the orchestra on such notable occasions as the first performance of Stravinsky's *The Rite of Spring* (although not, as the Seraphim liner note somewhat overenthusiastically claims, at the first performance of Debussy's *Prelude to "The Afternoon of a Faun"*—an event that took place when Moÿse was only five years old). After his retirement from his Paris posts, Moÿse joined Adolf Busch and Rudolf Serkin in founding the Marlboro Music School and Festival in Vermont.

In the 1930s, Moÿse had worked with Busch in a noted series of concerts and recordings devoted to the music of Bach. In their day, these performances were much acclaimed for, like Edwin Fischer, Busch pioneered the restoration of 18th-century music to its original small instrumental proportions and textural transparency. To appreciate their original impact, these recordings should be compared with earlier ones—say, the B minor Suite as played by the Amsterdam Concertgebouw Orchestra under Willem Mengelberg, with a body of strings so thick of tone that the solo flute line had frequently to be doubled to make it audible. No troubling hearing Moÿse—and the lively tempos and rhythmically poised phrasings also make more musical sense than Mengelberg's ponderosity, for they recognize the role of dance rhythms in Bach's instrumental works. The Busch ensembles prepared their performances as chamber music rather than as examples of orchestral discipline imposed by a conductor, and the players included many celebrated soloists. Still to come was the use of 18th-cen-

Marcel Moÿse, the dean of French flutists, has continued to train wind players and to conduct chamber ensembles, long after retiring from solo performance.

tury instruments; Busch did not even embrace the harpsichord, which was by the mid-1930s a familiar presence in London and Paris—the keyboard parts are played on the piano by Busch's son-in-law, Rudolf Serkin.

In the manuscript sources, Bach's Suites are actually headed by the name of the first movements: "Overture," a piece in the style of a French opera overture, with a slow opening section featuring dotted rhythms followed by a lively fugal section and a return to the opening tempo. The subsequent movements present a variety of dance styles in concert settings. Of Bach's four Suites for orchestra, the one in B minor for flute and strings is the most lightly scored; though the flute often simply doubles the violins, in several movements it is given a virtuosic solo role, which becomes at times as spectacular as the soloist's part in a concerto. Despite the dissimilarity of his instrument to the one for which Bach was writing, Moÿse makes a graceful effect with the fast passagework and wide skips of the "Double" (or Variation) on the Polonaise, and in the concluding Badinerie his catchy phrasing brings the music to vivid rhythmic life.

Typically, the Baroque concerto contrasts a small group of solo instruments (the *concertino*) against the full ensemble (the *ripieno*); the latter weighs in at important structural points, often with the principal thematic material (or *ritornello*), to confirm the arrival in a new key and, eventually, the return to the starting point. Each of Bach's six Brandenburg Concertos—so named because they were assembled in a set and presented in 1721 to the Margrave of Brandenburg, a German principality—features a different instrumental layout. In the Fifth Concerto, the concertino comprises flute, violin, and keyboard instrument (played on the piano in this recording); for the latter, there is an exceptionally elaborate part in the first movement, with a lengthy and showy cadenza that is presented by Serkin with sustained brilliance and tension in a somewhat Brahmsian style—the phrasing and articulation are decidedly pianistic, not at all imitative of the harpsichord.

The slow movement is for the concertino alone—a trio-sonata texture with much imitation among the parts, affording Moÿse, Busch, and Serkin opportunities to match phrasings in the best chamber-music style. The finale is a gigue in fugal style, at once learned and merry. In most of this performance, the clarity of ensemble, the audibility and vitality of the individual contrapuntal lines is admirable, but both first and third movements (as well as the first movement of the Suite) are unfortunately marred by side breaks in the original 78 RPM records where the tempo is not precisely maintained from one side to the next, so that a smooth edit appears to have been impossible. In the last movement of the Concerto, unfortunately, the problem is more than momentary, for after the splice the tempo becomes a bit ponderous and loses its initial vitality. A certain fussiness, too, results from Busch's insistence in the Gigue on making the upbeats of the principal subject shorter than the running notes that follow—which is in fact a misunderstanding of 18th-century notation, and one of the stylistic errors that more recent performers have learned to avoid. (The complete Busch set of Brandenburg Concertos is scheduled for reissue in the UK by World Records.)

It may well be that the overall shaping of Busch's performances, their directed sense of departure from and arrival at a destination, is essentially anachronistic, that 18th-century performances of this music were more "readings" and less "interpretations" than we have become accustomed to—but that the pieces make sense in Busch's terms (and that our ears easily hear them that way) is scarcely arguable. I have no doubt that these performances are more satisfying, in their lively and thoughtful musicianship, than many postwar exemplars of "sewing-machine" Baroque style such as the recordings of Karl Münchinger.

Unfortunately, very few of Marcel Moÿse's many recordings, principally for French labels, have been reissued. Of his colleagues in these Bach recordings, Rudolf Serkin has, of course, become one of the celebrated pianists of his generation, a performer of enormous musicianship and a nervous temperament that sometimes helps—but also sometimes mars—his interpretations; many of his stereo recordings are still in the catalogue. Of Adolf Busch, more in a later section.

LEON GOOSSENS
Oboe

Mozart: Quartet in F major for Oboe and Strings, K. 370 (with members of the Léner Quartet; recorded 1933)

UK :World Records SH-318 (with Mozart: Clarinet Quintet, played by Charles Draper and the Léner Quartet)

The Goossens family, of Belgian origin, furnished England with a number of distinguished musicians. Each of three generations had its Eugene Goossens and all three were conductors—the last of them, knighted in 1955 as Sir Eugene, was also a composer and was particularly active in the dissemination of contemporary music. Two of his sisters, Marie and Sidonie, were harpists, while a younger brother, Leon (b. 1897), became Britain's finest oboist. A member of various London orchestras (including Sir Thomas Beecham's prewar London Philharmonic), Leon Goossens also stimulated composers such as Ralph Vaughan Williams and Benjamin Britten to write important new works for the oboe. He was a significant figure in the development towards a sweeter, more tractable tone quality for his instrument, particularly through the increased use of vibrato.

The Quartet for Oboe and Strings in F major, which Mozart composed in 1781 for his friend the Munich oboist Friedrich Ramm, is one of the composer's lighter works, although demanding of the soloist in range and agility. Even the central Adagio, in D minor, is brief and restrained, while the outer movements are sunny throughout. (At one point in the last movement, presumably as a joke on Ramm, Mozart sets the oboe at odds with the prevailing six-beat rhythm, making him fit four beats to the strings' six.)

Leon Goossens, the leading British oboist of modern times, helped to improve the instrument's technique and tone, as well as commissioning works that expanded its repertoire.

From the spring of the very first upbeat, Goossens gives the Quartet a spinning forward motion, carrying the string players successfully with him—a pleasant surprise, for the playing of the Léner Quartet on records is often erratic and shapeless (for example, in the coupled Clarinet Quintet). The oboist's articulation is always precise and vivacious, his intonation generally consistent (the final notes unfortunately go a shade on the flat side), the whole an invigorating ensemble.

Goossens sustained serious damage to his mouth in a 1962 automobile accident, but was able to reconstruct his technique, as confirmed in a late recital disk (UK: RCA RL-25142). Shortly before the accident, he recorded Bach and Handel concertos with Yehudi Menuhin (US: Angel S-36103; UK: EMI/HMV SXLP-30294). Particularly attractive is a collection of earlier concerto recordings (UK: World Records SH-243), containing the concerto written for Goossens by Vaughan Williams, the Richard Strauss concerto (the only recording to preserve the original, more compact ending, which Strauss elaborated later into the published version), and an arrangement for oboe d'amore (an alto oboe) and strings of a Bach keyboard concerto (made by Sir Donald Tovey, on the widely accepted assumption that the keyboard piece is Bach's own arrangement of a lost original for another instrument). And of course Goossens's playing enhances the many recordings made before World War II by Sir Thomas Beecham and the London Philharmonic—for example, the later Mozart Symphonies (US: Turnabout THS-65022/6; UK: World Records SHB-20, five disks).

DENNIS BRAIN
Horn

*Mozart: Concertos for Horn and Orchestra: No. 1 in D major, K. 412 • No.
2 in E-flat major, K. 417 • No. 3 in E-flat major, K. 447 • No. 4 in E-flat
major, K. 495 (with the Philharmonia Orchestra, conducted by Herbert von
Karajan; recorded 1953)*

US: Angel 35092; UK: EMI/HMV ASD-1140, electronic stereo

Another celebrated musical family in Britain was the
Brains, who for three generations produced the country's leading horn players: A.E. Brain, his sons Alfred
and Aubrey, and Aubrey's son Dennis (another of Aubrey's sons, Leonard, was a prominent oboist). Dennis
Brain (1921–1957) was one of those prodigies who ad-
vance the standards of performance on an instrument.
He achieved a level of facility, flexibility, and security previously associated with more tractable instruments such
as the clarinet, and his perfectly formed and controlled
mouth hardly ever let pass a suspicion of the "split
notes" that are traditionally the bane of the hornist's ex-
istence. Just as Roger Bannister's breaking of the four-
minute-mile barrier released the energies of many other
runners, so Dennis Brain stimulated younger players to
raise their standards. After making his debut in 1938, at
the age of seventeen, alongside his father in a Busch performance of Bach's First Brandenburg Concerto, Dennis
Brain spent the war in an RAF band and then joined the
newly formed Philharmonia Orchestra, where he remained until his tragic death in an auto accident in 1957.
At that time, his career in solo work had been steadily
growing, and it seems likely that he would eventually
have been able to concentrate on that repertoire.

At the center of the Classical horn literature stand Mozart's three concertos in E-flat major (the Concerto in D is
actually two unrelated movements that somehow were
spliced together—one of musicology's minor mysteries),
written for Joseph Leutgeb, a friend of the Mozart family
and a considerable virtuoso in his day. Leutgeb played,
of course, on the valveless or "natural" horn, which
could produce far fewer notes than the modern instrument (and some of those could only be made by stuffing
the hand in the bell of the horn to lower the pitch).

Dennis Brain, the prodigious horn player, who in his short career proved that the instrument could be played with more security and fluency that anyone had ever dreamed possible.

Though easier to play on today's valved horn, Mozart's concertos demand great poise and fluency.

Essentially occasional pieces, of low density and tension, the concertos present few formal problems aside from the occasional altered sequence of themes in recapitulation, or such niceties as the contrasting theme in the Rondo of K. 447, which recalls the principal melody of the slow movement. The concertos are cut from pretty much the same cloth, especially in the hunting-call style of the final movements, and they are probably best served by being heard one at a time, as Mozart surely intended them to be, rather than in the sequence imposed by the LP record.

Brain's mastery is as self-evident as Mozart's. The unruffled security of the playing, the rounded, homogeneous tone, the technical fluency in scales, arpeggios, trills, and skips, the variety of tonal color ranging from the inward tone of the slow movements to the brash outdoor sound of the finales—all can be immediately and directly enjoyed. So, too, can the musicianship: the firm and robust rhythmic feeling, the deftly shaded phrases, the soloist's ability to match perfectly the most delicate articulations by other instruments of the orchestra when repeating a phrase. If I had to pick a single passage to exemplify Brain's instrumental command and musical sensitivity, it might be the second contrasting episode in the Rondo of K. 417, which begins with incredibly light, fanfarelike repeated notes on the horn and continues with a series of relatively unmelodious phrases for the soloist that Brain invests with so much light and shade, such subtle contrasts and gentle releases, that they remain forever fixed in the mind.

Brain frequently argued that good horn tone was a property of the player, not of the instrument, and on several occasions provided a convincing demonstration of that proposition when he played with his horn mouthpiece on a length of ordinary garden hose! Two recorded examples of this feat survive, one on an enjoyable disk that includes spoken reminiscences by his colleagues, some excerpts from Brain's BBC talks, and portions of his final concert appearance in 1957 (US: Arabesque 8071; UK: BBC Artium REGL-352); the other is part of that *locus classicus* of musical humor, the first "Hoffnung Music Festival," at which he played a movement from a concerto by Mozart's father on the hose—and also played the organ, an instrument on which he apparently could have had an equally successful career (US: Angel 35500; UK: EMI/HMV SLS-5069, three disks).

There are a number of significant Brain recordings, although hardly enough. The two concertos by Richard Strauss (whose father was a great horn player in Munich in Wagner's day) are highly recommended (US: Angel 35496; UK: EMI/HMV HLS-7001). Among the works written especially for Brain are the Hindemith Horn Concerto (US: Angel S-35491; UK: EMI/HMV HSL-7001; conducted by the composer), and Britten's *Serenade for Tenor, Horn and Strings* (which Brain recorded twice; the original 1944–45 version, with Peter Pears singing and Britten conducting, is available on UK: Decca/Eclipse ECM-814). On an interesting collection of recordings ranging from 1944 to 1953, we can hear both the French instrument that Brain used during the earlier part of his career and the more robust-toned and flexible British instrument that he changed to in 1951 (US: Seraphim 60040); this disk includes an earlier version of the Mozart Concerto, K. 417 played on the French instrument, which allows a direct comparison with the later, more familiar recording. Two additional Seraphim disks present Brain's work with various chamber ensembles (US: Seraphim 60073, 60169), though not, unfortunately, in that central work of the hornist's chamber repertoire, Brahms's great Trio in E-flat. A broadcast recording of the Brahms (UK: BBC REB-175), valuable as a souvenir of Brain's virtuosity.

playing, and not a simple one, for there are many subtle refinements. The best players often "bend" notes—for example, edging a note slightly towards its successor when a harmonic and melodic resolution is involved. This freedom to adjust pitch is one of the expressive strengths of the string instrument, though it ought not to be overdone. Another significant aspect of violin tone is *vibrato*, the slight vibration imparted to the pitch by a fast oscillation of the finger that is creating the note, giving the tone a warm, almost vocal quality.

All notes except the lowest and the highest can be played on any of several strings, and many considerations enter into the choice of string. The different strings have different tonal qualities, ranging from the dark, almost throaty G string to the brightness of the E string, and it may be musically desirable, say, to keep a melody on one string and in one color. If a melody involves a big skip, there is a choice between shifting to another string or shifting the hand position—which will entail sliding the finger along the string and creating in the process the sliding sound known as portamento. (Frequent in the 19th century, the constant use of portamento has gradually gone out of fashion during the 20th, and modern violinists have found ways of reducing its use.) Often the options for fingering a passage present a choice between simplicity and musicality: one will be safer, more reliable, the other will yield a better phrasing or apter expressive character.

Bowing Techniques

Bowing presents another host of complexities. Downward strokes of the bow can more comfortably be made loud and forceful, and so are often preferred for downbeats and in playing vigorous music. But an uninterrupted series of down-strokes is hardly possible, for the player soon reaches the end of the bow. So a fairly regular alternation of down and up is necessary, its exact details often affected by the fact that louder notes will usually be played with faster bow strokes, which use up more bow than softer notes of the same duration. There are many different types of bow strokes, described by such terms as "hammered," "jumping," "thrown," for different kinds of articulation. In fast staccato writing it is possible to bounce the bow on the strings with particularly lively effect. Other variables include the amount of bowhair used against the string, and the point along the string at which the bow is applied—closer to the bridge means a louder tone.

Nor do the possibilities of bowing exhaust the many kinds of sound and articulation available to a string player. He can also pluck the strings (*pizzicato*). By bowing on the fingerboard, he can get a very soft tone; by bowing very close to the bridge, a glassy tone; by bowing with the wood of the bow rather than the horsehair, a wraithlike effect with very little tone at all. A mute placed on the bridge will result in subdued tone. By gently touching the string at its half, third, quarter, and other equal divisions, partials or *harmonics* can be sounded, very clear and pure. Finally, there are multiple stops: two notes can be sounded simultaneously if they are played on adjacent strings, and the effect of chords of three or four notes can be obtained by passing the bow across more strings. Double stops are particularly common in virtuoso writing, and a significant literature of music for solo violin—notably six celebrated sonatas by Bach—relies on such chordal possibilities to rear extraordinary musical structures on the slender foundation of four strings and a bow.

The Violin's Evolution

Both the instrument and its technique have changed much over the centuries. The most famous violins are those built by a group of Italians between 1650 and 1750: Stradivari, Amati, Guarneri. All of their instruments, however, were significantly modified during the 19th century to produce a tone powerful enough to fill modern halls, and to accommodate such features as a chin rest. Furthermore, modern violinists play these instruments with 19th-century French bows. The original gut strings have long since been replaced by strings wound with wire and, since the early 20th century, the violin's E string has usually been made of steel—more reliable and brilliant than gut, though perhaps at a sacrifice of tonal sweetness. (The recent revival of period instruments for the performance of 18th-century music gives us a chance again to hear the sound of gut strings at lower tension.)

The muscular control demanded in string playing is extraordinary, and exceptional in that the two hands and arms must acquire quite different kinds of mastery—a kind of asymmetrical coordination not required of keyboard or wind players. In recompense, the great string player commands a remarkable expressive capability;

the tone of the instrument can be varied and colored as flexibly as the human voice, can surpass it in sheer virtuosity and in staying power.

FRITZ KREISLER
Violin

"FRITZ KREISLER SOUVENIRS"

Kreisler: Tambourin chinois; Caprice viennois • Gypsy Caprice • Shepherd's Madrigal • Schön Rosmarin • Liebesleid • Liebesfreud • The Old Refrain • Chanson Louis XIII and Pavane (in the style of Couperin) • Dohnányi (arr. Kreisler): Ruralia Hungarica—Gypsy Andante • Dvořák (arr. Kreisler): Humoresque • Sonatina, Op. 100—2nd movement ("Indian Lament") • Slavonic Dances: Op. 46, No. 2 and Op. 72, No. 8 (with Carl Lamson, piano; recorded 1924-29)

US: **RCA Victrola VIC-1372**

One of the more remarkable prodigies, the Austrian violinist Fritz Kreisler (1875-1962) entered the Vienna Conservatory at the age of seven and received the school's gold medal three years later. Two years at the Paris Conservatory completed his musical studies, after which he returned to Vienna for a premedical education and military service, only taking up the violin again in 1896. The hiatus apparently caused no problems, and his career quickly became international, centering in Berlin and Vienna. After the German annexation of Austria, Kreisler came to the US (his wife was American) and acquired citizenship in 1943. He continued to play in public and on the radio until the late 1940s, though an accident in 1941 impaired his sight and hearing.

Kreisler combined technical mastery with an exceptional charm and elegance of musicianship, and his tone had an unprecedented beauty and expressiveness. Earlier violinists of the French school had used vibrato in slow music, but Kreisler was the first to extend its use to fast passages as well, giving them a new warmth and color. Kreisler elicited many tributes, among them a major concerto written with his playing in mind—the English composer Edward Elgar's concerto—which, alas, Kreisler never recorded.

To the fiddler's repertoire, Kreisler made direct contributions as well, including his grand and much-played cadenzas for the Beethoven and Brahms Violin Con-

Fritz Kreisler, the great Viennese violinist, whose sweet tone and passionate interpretations made a sensation in the musical world at the beginning of the 20th century.

certos and a large number of short character pieces and transcriptions for the violin. Reluctant to have his name appear too often on his programs, Kreisler ascribed some of his original pieces to 18th-century composers; later, when the deception was unmasked, some critics made a rather silly fuss. These pieces are now billed as "in the style of . . ." and are still played, though as we have come to know more 18th-century music, their inauthenticity has become more glaring. In general, Kreisler's less pretentious pieces, mostly in the Viennese and Hungarian-gypsy styles, have retained the greatest popularity, and every violinist worth his salt has recorded a clutch of them.

Kreisler himself recorded many of his pieces several times, but the recordings of the 1920s, when he was about fifty years old, are preferable to the later ones from the late 1930s and the even less successful ones from the 1940s; the playing on the earlier, accoustically recorded ones is excellent, but the sound leaves a great deal to be desired. (The present version of *The Old Refrain*, Kreisler's arrangement of a Viennese song, was acoustically recorded in 1924, but the other performances on the Victrola disk are electrical recordings.)

Usually in simple ternary (ABA) form, Kreisler's pieces are not virtuoso stunts of extreme difficulty; they are principally vehicles for his own particular virtues of warm tone and graceful phrasing, while exploiting all the resources of the violin. Double stops are used frequently (for example, the principal melody of *Caprice viennois*, in thirds, and the repetition of *The Old Refrain*, in sixths). Some high notes are played as harmonics, as, for example, the final phrase of the Dvořák transcription known as *Indian Lament*. The special richness of the G string is frequently exploited (the first statement of *The Old Refrain*, for example), and the melancholy of *Liebesleid* (Love's Sorrow) is underlined by playing most of it one string lower than would be normal. Pizzicato is used sparingly, as at the end of the first section of *Tambourin chinois* and in the central section of *Caprice viennois*, which is also an excellent example of bouncing, *spiccato* bowing. The low note to which the first phrase of *Tambourin chinois* plunges is the open (that is, unfingered) G string, and Kreisler justifies its obviously different tone color by making it an accented point of destination rather than just some secondary note that unavoidably sticks out. (The other open-string notes can be avoided by playing them as stopped notes on a lower string, but there is no other way to play the low G.)

Once the listener has observed some of these aspects of violin technique in action, he will be increasingly aware of Kreisler's very personal style: his tone, of course, and the vibrato that enlivens it; his natural, never laggard sense of rhythm and forward motion; and his frequent, never exaggerated use of rubato (though it is also a Kreisler mannerism sometimes to rush passage-work at the ends of phrases, building to the next down-beat). His regular use of portamento is very much a part of the Central European popular idiom in which most of this music is cast. (Kreisler, a Viennese, is especially fond of slow waltzes with cross-rhythms—in which, for example, the melody will have three strong accents during the time that the oom-pah-pah, oom-pah-pah accompaniment will have only two.) Listening to Kreisler's phrasing and articulation, one discovers he does not use that portamento indiscriminately; notice in *Caprice viennois* how often the bow is lifted from the strings, how the melody is articulated into natural segments.

At times the subtlety and variety of Kreisler's articulation seems to approach that of human speech; the figuration of his *Gypsy Caprice*, for example, is made remarkably absorbing by the changing colors, dynamics, and attacks that Kreisler's bow draws from the strings. A special case is the *Chanson Louis XIII and Pavane*, one of the 18th-century pastiches, played in a self-consciously "pure" style with steady, even semi-detached, bowing, but Kreisler's trademarks are nonetheless present—in the Pavane, the tendency to rush faster notes, and, at the end, an unmistakable portamento signature.

The distinctiveness of Kreisler's violinistic personality is thrown into sharp relief by any comparison with the work of other violinists. Try Szigeti playing *Liebesleid* (in the Szigeti set considered below): stiffer and heavier rhythmically, more wiry of tone, and in total effect slightly grim, which cannot be right. Heifetz, on the other hand, in his 1920 recording of the Slavonic Dance, Op. 72, No. 8 (US: RCA Red Seal ARM4-0942, four disks) or his 1934 version of the Dohnányi *Gypsy Andante* (US: RCA Red Seal ARM4-0943, four disks), offers a bigger, richer tone and a broader, showier manner, but nothing like the fine detail, intimate elegance, or spirit of fantasy that makes Kreisler's readings so personal.

By the time electrical recording came along, Kreisler was already fifty, and it is unfortunately true that not many recordings of major works represent him at his best. His earlier versions, conducted by Leo Blech, of the concertos of Beethoven (UK: EMI/HMV HLM-7062; G: EMI/Electrola C-047-01243), Brahms (G: EMI/Electrola C-053-01410), and Mendelssohn (UK: Pearl GEMM-190) are better than the later ones from the mid-1930s, but, despite many beauties of detail, even these don't add up to the kind of coherent statements that later recordings by other violinists would provide. Not currently available, but not to be missed if they are reissued, are several earlier editions of the violin sonatas that Kreisler recorded with Sergei Rachmaninoff on piano: the performances of Beethoven's Sonata in G major, Op. 30, No. 3, Grieg's Sonata No. 3 in C minor, and Schubert's Sonata in A major, D. 574 are remarkable dialogues between two strong and distinctive musical personalities. (Later in the 1930s, Kreisler recorded all of the Beethoven Violin Sonatas with Franz Rupp for HMV, but the partnership is rather one-sided and the violin playing no longer secure.) A close musical friend of both Kreisler and Rachmaninoff was the tenor John McCormack, with whom Kreisler recorded a number of Rachmaninoff's songs—performances in which the violin obbligato parts are no less specific and expressive than the vocal lines (all of the Mc-Cormack-Kreisler collaborations, including quite a bit of kitsch, are included in UK: Pearl GEMM-155/60, six disks, an excellent cross-section of McCormack's hundreds of recordings).

JOSEPH SZIGETI
Violin

"THE ART OF JOSEPH SZIGETI"

Bach: Concerto in D minor, after BWV 1052 (with the Orchestra of the New Friends of Music, conducted by Fritz Stiedry (recorded 1940) • Sonata No. 1 in G minor, BWV 1001 (recorded 1931) • Partita No. 3 in E major, BWV 1006—Praeludium (recorded 1908) • Handel: Sonata in D major, Op. 1, No. 15 (with Nikita Magaloff, piano; recorded 1937) • Beethoven: Sonatas No. 5 in F major, Op. 24 ("Spring") and No. 10 in G major, Op. 96 (with Artur Schnabel, piano; recorded at concert, 1948) • Concerto in D major, Op. 61 (with the British Symphony Orchestra, conducted by Bruno Walter; recorded 1932) • Mozart: Concerto No. 4 in D major, K. 218 (with the London Philharmonic Orchestra, conducted by Sir Thomas Beecham; recorded 1934) • Mendelssohn: Concerto in E minor, Op. 64 (with the London Philharmonic Orchestra, conducted by Sir Thomas Beecham; recorded 1933) • Brahms: Concerto in D major. Op. 77 (with the Hallé Orchestra, conducted by Sir Hamilton Harty; recorded 1928) • Prokofiev: Concerto No. 1 in D major, Op. 19 (with the London Philharmonic Orchestra, conducted by Sir Thomas Beecham; recorded 1935) • Dvořák (arr. Kreisler): Slavonic Dance, Op. 72, No. 2 (with Magaloff; recorded 1926) • Kreisler: Liebesleid (with Magaloff; recorded 1933) • Rimsky-Korsakov: Flight of the Bumblebee (with Magaloff; recorded 1933) • Bartók: Hungarian Folk Tunes; Roumanian Folk Dances (with Béla Bartók, piano; recorded 1930)

US: CBS Columbia M6X-31513, six disks

Joseph Szigeti (1892–1973), though he began his career early like most violinists, eventually became something other than a traditional virtuoso. From the 1920s until his gradual retirement in the 1960s, Szigeti was regarded as a "musician's violinist," as distinct from those like Heifetz who were "violinists' violinists." Not that Szigeti couldn't play the violin (although some aspects of his technique, formed under Jenö Hubay at the Budapest Conservatory, were regarded as old-fashioned and inhibiting)—but the focus of interest in his performances was always the music rather than the instrument.

Szigeti actively worked at the expansion of the repertoire, reviving older works and advocating new ones. At a time when only single movements from the Bach solo sonatas were regarded as acceptable recital fare, he played the works complete—and his playing of them inspired his older colleague, the great Belgian violinist Ysaÿe, to compose his own solo violin sonatas, the first of which is dedicated to Szigeti. The concertos of Sir Hamilton Harty, Alfred Casella, and Frank Martin are dedicated to Szigeti, who also established Prokofiev's First Concerto in the Western repertoire.

The tribute that Columbia assembled for Szigeti's eightieth birthday is an admirable compilation, including concertos, chamber music, an unaccompanied Bach sonata, and encore pieces (one of them recorded when the violinist was sixteen). To discuss them all is precluded by reasons of space; we will return later to Szigeti as a chamber-music player, so let us concentrate here on the concertos. Only the Bach arrangement—another of those reconstructions of a hypothetical original from which Bach supposedly made a keyboard concerto—is disappointing, rough in tone and showing the advent of technical problems that would dog Szigeti (as many other violinists) after his fiftieth year. The Mozart Concerto in D, on the other hand, is played with great security and much vigorous articulation.

The grandest of violin concertos is Beethoven's—also one of the most difficult to bring off convincingly, for the solo writing, full of even scales and arpeggios, can easily seem bland, unworthy of the splendid orchestral material. In the first movement, the orchestral exposition is indeed one of Beethoven's most spacious, but overtones of urgency, even militance, are implicit in the drum beats that precede the principal subject in the winds. (Those repeated notes, sometimes in the timpani but more often elsewhere, appear more than seventy times during the movement to introduce suggestions of restlessness, suspense, menace, and eventually celebration; it is worth devoting a hearing of the movement simply to tracking down this motive in all its manifestations.) Then the violins take up the taps, on a harmonically ambiguous note that is not resolved directly at this point and remains a question mark. After some scales in the winds, the orchestra abruptly bursts out in a distant key, a pivotal passage that will return at unexpected places and that here leads to the second subject, again in the winds and again lyrical. This is developed at some length, beginning in a minor key and leading to a brief allusion to the ambiguous note and then to a climax followed by a new, rising theme and a cadence (a closing formula).

The clinching chord of that cadence is withheld, however, and the solo violin enters, ascending in octaves to a high point, from which it then descends in the even passagework that becomes its basic vocabulary. It is a splendid entrance, though absolutely dependent for its effect on the violinist's security in those ascending octaves; Szi-

Joseph Szigeti, whose eloquent performances of classic and modern violin concertos remain touchstones of style and musicianship after nearly half a century.

geti does not fail us here. The second exposition now follows in orderly sequence, skipping only the abrupt orchestral outburst. The closing theme is extended at some length and then the violin again ascends to a great height, settling on a trill that is nudged by the drum taps higher and higher; we seem to be on the verge of a conclusion to this section.

Instead, the big orchestral outburst interrupts and leads us to the second subject again, this time without the soloist. A broad modulation deflects us to music from the end of the orchestral exposition, now in a new key, followed by the re-entrance of the soloist with his ascending octaves. The first subject now appears in a minor key, developed by a pair of bassoons as the violin ranges around in rapid figuration. While the horns solemnly beat out the repeated-note figure, the violin plays characteristic rising phrases, soon turning radiantly to a major key (here Szigeti gently underlines the great event). The repeated notes gradually subside and then reenter as the violin starts climbing upwards, and then the full orchestra hammers out the drum taps, introducing the recapitulation.

Like the second exposition, this initially evades the big orchestral outburst, reserving it for the end, where it this time leads to a cadenza. Szigeti plays the cadenza written by Brahms's violinist friend Joachim, which features strong double stops (Beethoven himself uses these only briefly, in the third movement of his concerto). Much is made of the drum-tap motive and of the theme of the big orchestral outburst, neither of which has been assigned to the violin during the movement proper. After the cadenza, the solo violin plays the second subject serenely on the lowest strings, and the closing theme makes a cadence.

For the violinist, the challenge of this movement—superbly met by Szigeti—is to shape the long stretches of rhythmically even scales and broken chords into coherent, shaped phrases, to articulate them with a variety of color and character that will define their formal and expressive function. Although Bruno Walter does not drive the tempo forward as aggressively as some conductors, the movement never lags, for it is always purposefully shaped and firmly rhythmed.

The slow second movement achieves its uncanny repose in an unusual way: it never changes key. Principally a set of variations, it avoids monotony because the theme makes a wide, if quickly resolved, modulation. The theme is stated first by strings, repeated by horns and clarinet with a violin commentary in a high register, again by bassoon with a more elaborate commentary, and finally in a rich, more forceful version for orchestra. Now the violin quietly explores some scales and introduces an entirely new melody, leading to a fourth variation, the violin again floating on high over pizzicato strings. Further rumination on the new melody, over fragments of the theme, reaches the vanishing point as a new variation seems to be under way, when suddenly the orchestra interrupts—undoubtedly the only way to end a piece that has never really budged from its home key and in which, therefore, the usual sense of closure created by a return to the home key can hardly be brought into play.

This slow movement challenges the poise of the violinist, for each phrase must be inflected with a clear yet not overly forceful sense of what is upbeat, what is downbeat. Too much stress anywhere would violate the dreamlike character, yet there must be enough accent to generate rhythmic shape, to maintain a sense of motion even when the orchestra comes to temporary stops so that the violin may soar. One might wish Szigeti were not quite so close to the microphone, and the proximity of the London Underground to the Central Hall, West-minster, where the recording was made, is occasionally evident, but the concentration of the playing is palpable. For the end of the movement, Joachim wrote two cadenzas; Szigeti wisely plays the one that devotes most of its brief course to anticipating the next movement rather than further reflecting on the previous one.

The third-movement rondo is played with great buoyancy, and again Szigeti negotiates long stretches of passagework in a musically lively and fascinating way. Like the first movement, this one includes a central episode in G minor in which the bassoon figures prominently—one of several interesting reflections between the two movements—and the bounce of Szigeti's flying arpeggios is particularly engaging. The coda after the cadenza (Joachim's again) begins with a harmonic excursion that affords this jovial movement something of the spaciousness of the others, before moving to the conclusion.

In his Violin Concerto, Felix Mendelssohn did away with double exposition: the soloist enters right away with the principal theme and remains at the fore throughout—a simplification of concerto form that found much favor with the virtuosos who subsequently composed display pieces with orchestra. Few of them managed to invest their concertos with the combination of charm, grace, and substance that Mendelssohn achieves here, although his other innovations—the first-movement cadenza (composed rather than left for improvisation) placed between development and recapitulation, and the transitional passages that bind together the three movements—were also often imitated. Szigeti's intonation is a bit less consistent than in the Beethoven and his tone less suave than that of some of his colleagues, but his variety of color and articulation is once again fascinating.

Szigeti's Brahms performance is admirable in many of the same ways as is his Beethoven, although his powerfully analytic readings of the passagework are not as crucial here because Brahms has already made the writing more directly related to the thematic substance. Even so, Szigeti's playing of the repeated little rhythmic figure in the later part of the first movement's development is wonderfully various, and he surmounts with power the obstacle course for the soloist that follows it and leads to the recapitulation: trills, arpeggios, wide skips, and octaves. He plays the cadenza of Joachim, Brahms's advisor on technical matters in the composition of the concerto.

The long oboe solo that begins the slow movement is one of the weaker moments in the Szigeti recording, although it makes an interesting comparison with the playing of Leon Goossens—this is definitely a pre-Goossens oboist, using no vibrato and producing a flat, woody tone with a suggestion of quack not far away. Szigeti's phrasing of the violin variant of this theme is sure and spacious, and when the music broadens after the briefly tempestuous central section he achieves a grand effect, withholding a true downbeat until the last possible moment. The Hungarian material of the finale is played with great brio, and the marchlike coda builds irresistibly. (The brief cadenzas in this movement were written out by Brahms.) Throughout, Sir Hamilton Harty provides a powerful orchestral framework.

Although Szigeti did not give the first performance of Prokofiev's D major Concerto, he early became its most eloquent exponent, both in the West and on tours to the Soviet Union, and it remains one his greatest achievements. Hearing it, one is tempted to suggest that Prokofiev and Szigeti between them invented a new kind of violin, for in this performance the sound of the piece is as distinctive, as untraditional as what Prokofiev achieved in his treatment of the piano. Some of it is, of course, in Prokofiev's score: the frequent use of harmonics, trills, pizzicatos—even at one point, strumming the violin like a banjo! But it was Szigeti who brought the implications of these devices to bear on the totality of the solo part; for example, the mysterious, almost whispered color of the opening prefigures the quality that this theme will assume when it returns at the end of the piece, each note now a trill. The raspy trills, the skaty, squealing, grotesque noises in the Scherzo, the throaty staccato in its middle section—all these are special sounds, quite unlike the almost human cantabile of the familiar instrument, which puts in a brief and surprising appearance at the beginning of the third movement. Although this is not musical territory normally associated with Sir Thomas Beecham, he and the London Philharmonic keep up admirably with the soloist.

Szigeti recorded one other contemporary concerto while in his prime, that of Ernest Bloch (US: Turnabout THS-65007). In the US in the 1940s, he rerecorded the Beethoven and Brahms concertos, but by then his technique had begun to slip. Late in the 1950s, he again recorded those two concertos and the Prokofiev in stereo, but these are strictly for the dedicated. Quite a few broadcast and concert recordings are floating around on labels such as that of the Bruno Walter Society but these, too, are mostly from the 1940s and 1950s. (Szigeti's chamber music recordings are discussed in the next chapter.)

JASCHA HEIFETZ
Violin

Silbelius: Violin Concerto in D minor, Op. 27 (with the London Philharmonic Orchestra, conducted by Sir Thomas Beecham; recorded 1935)

US: Seraphim 60221 (with Tchaikovsky: Violin Concerto); UK: World Records SH-207 (with other Sibelius works, conducted by Beecham and Sibelius)

The most celebrated pupil of Leopold Auer, the Hungarian-born violin professor at the St. Petersburg conservatory, was Jascha Heifetz (b. 1901). Heifetz made a spectacular Berlin debut in 1912, and in 1917 he came to the US on his first tour. A famous anecdote is told of his Carnegie Hall debut: the Viennese pianist and wit Moriz Rosenthal was sitting in the audience with a violinist colleague, who halfway through the concert whispered, "It's hot in here"—to which Rosenthal replied, "Not for pianists." For the next several decades, Heifetz, who settled in the US, stood as the paragon of technical perfection among string players. Although he greatly reduced his public appearances in the 1950s and 1960s, occasional emergences from retirement showed that his powers were still intact (a 1972 recital was published as US: Columbia M2-33444, two disks).

Characteristic of Heifetz (and of earlier Auer pupils such as Mischa Elman and Efrem Zimbalist) is a bigger tone than that used by Kreisler, Szigeti, and other Western players. With a heavier bow pressure, tauter bowstrings, more use of the lower strings, and a bigger vibrato, the Russian violinists produced a more powerful and intense violin sound than had been heard before. This tone was more naturally suited to the Slavic expressivity of Tchaikovsky than to the Classical serenity of Mozart, but the best of these players found ample response to their playing of a wide repertoire.

Jascha Heifetz, the greatest master of the violin in modern times and for more than fifty years the paragon of virtuoso string playing.

Among them, Heifetz was clearly the most accomplished technically, and he also proved to be the most controlled expressively. So much so, in fact, that his interpretations often earned adjectives such as "cold," "slick," and "superficial." The great violinist and teacher Carl Flesch suggested that "the absolute infallibility of his technical apparatus is his worst enemy because it promotes a certain emotional inertia. . . . People would forgive Heifetz his technical infallibility only if he would make them forget it by putting his entire personality behind it." Perhaps sensing that his full personality would not sit comfortably in the great Classical concertos, Heifetz frequently offers little in its place except his instrumental perfection—and the results can be (in Bernard Shaw's famous phrase about the singer Nellie Melba) "uninterestingly perfect and perfectly uninteresting."

An exception, by unanimous agreement, is the Sibelius Violin Concerto, where Heifetz's complete commitment is unmistakable. The first movement, in the loose, post-Mendelssohn style, introduces three principal subject groups. The first is for the soloist, who enters strikingly on a dissonant note and extends his rhapsodic melody. After a violin cadenza, the second group involves several related themes, the last in broad double stops for the soloist. The third group is for orchestra alone, beginning vigorously and eventually collapsing into the depths. Instead of a development section (or, more accurately, in addition to the development that these themes have already undergone), the pivotal place in the movement is occupied by a solo cadenza, after which the themes return in order and in new instrumental garbs.

Early on, we encounter characteristic gesture of the solo violin in this concerto, an upward sweep from low to high register—sometimes an arpeggio, sometimes a scale, sometimes in double stops (thirds or octaves). Heifetz not only maintains impeccable intonation in such phrases, but also intensity of tone, which glows as much in the quick figuration as in the slow opening melody of the movement. And these slashing upward phrases are attacked with such daring abandon, such perfect confidence; you can hear the portamento as the left hand slides up to high positions on the E string, and there is never any hesitation about stopping at precisely the right place.

In the slow movement, the principal melody, first played on the violin's G string, brings out the intensity in another dimension. After a brief and stormy intermezzo, the orchestra takes up the big melody, with the soloist offering eloquent counterpoints and, at the end, taking over the final phrases. The third movement is a vigorous and distinctive rondo, the main theme of which was aptly described by the great analyst Sir Donald Tovey as a "polonaise for polar bears" (the principal contrasting section, with its cross-rhythm, must be a dance for three-legged polar bears!). Here the violin races up and down, leading the orchestra a chase more intense than merry, and the combination of energy and accuracy in Heifetz's playing, as well as the vividly varied articulation, is nothing short of demonic. It is one of those special cases where a work and a performer appear to be perfectly matched, and the result makes every other performance of the Sibelius Concerto seem to fall short.

More of Heifetz's recordings are currently available than those of any other violinist, thanks to an elaborate series of reissues undertaken by RCA in honor of his seventy-fifth birthday, republishing nearly all of his pre-stereo recordings not then available; regardless of one's reactions to Heifetz's interpretations, this remarkable series is a major document in the history of violin-playing. In six volumes (US: RCA Red Seal ARM-0942/7, four disks each), "The Heifetz Collection" proceeds more or less chronologically from 1917 acoustical recordings of

encore pieces to concertos and sonatas taped in the early
1950s. Perhaps the most interesting set is Volume 4
(ARM-0945), containing concerto recordings from the
years before World War II: the Beethoven conducted by
Toscanini, the Brahms and Prokofiev Second by Kous-
sevitzky, the Brahms Double Concerto with Emanuel
Feuermann, and the concerto that William Walton composed for Heifetz.

A supplementary set devoted to chamber music (US:
RCA Red Seal CRM6-02264; UK: RCA RL-42474, six
disks) is particularly valuable for trios with Primrose,
Feuermann, and Piatigorsky. Other readily available
Heifetz mono recordings are his postwar versions of the
Mozart Concerto No. 4 in D major, K. 218 and the Mendelssohn, conducted by Beecham (US: Seraphim 60162;
UK: the Mendelssohn only, in World Records SHB-100,
eight discs, the Beecham centennial box). A very high-
powered performance of Franck's Violin Sonata, with
Artur Rubinstein, is coupled with the Bach Partita in D
minor (US: Seraphim 60230). And Heifetz's stereo versions of the major concertos are still listed in the current
catalogues in various couplings.

Everything in the Heifetz recorded repertoire is
violinistically impressive, and here and there a work
seems to capture the soloist's imagination in the way of
the Sibelius Concerto: for example, Bruch's lovely *Scot-
tish Fantasy*, of which Heifetz's was the first recording
ever (in ARM4-0946). But the absence of personal involvement, mentioned earlier, is more common, and often Heifetz engages the music only on the technical level,
with results that can be fussy. Still, the consistency of
Heifetz's achievement on recordings from 1917 to 1972—a
span of fifty-five years—is something to wonder at.

YEHUDI MENUHIN
Violin

*Elgar: Violin Concerto in B minor, Op. 61 (with the London Symphony
Orchestra, conducted by Sir Edward Elgar; recorded 1932)*
UK: **EMI/HMV HLM-7107**

Many child prodigies have been wildly acclaimed for
their mastery of instrumental technique, but few have
received such unqualified admiration for the maturity of

Yehudi Menuhin, the most famous child prodigy of the century, matured into a musician of integrity and imagination.

their musical conceptions as Yehudi Menuhin (b. 1916). Born in New York and raised in San Francisco, where he studied with the remarkable violinist and pianist Louis Persinger, Menuhin made a debut in Paris before his eleventh birthday. Later the same year, he played the pinnacle of the violin literature, the Beethoven Concerto, with the New York Philharmonic under Fritz Busch (the conductor had opposed the choice of concerto—"One does not hire Jackie Coogan to play Hamlet"—but changed his mind when he heard the boy play). Further studies with Adolf Busch and with the Rumanian composer and violinist Georges Enescu followed, while Menuhin pursued his career. His first recordings were made in 1928, and the following year he recorded an astonishingly powerful performance of Bach's Sonata in C major for solo violin.

For years Fred Gaisberg, HMV's recording manager, had tried to arrange a recording of Sir Edward Elgar's Violin Concerto, with the composer conducting and Fritz Kreisler, to whom the work is dedicated, as soloist. The plan never worked out, and in 1932, fearful that time was running out on the seventy-five-year-old Elgar, Gaisberg proposed Menuhin as soloist. The result was another remarkable performance, particularly impressive because this was not a frequently played work, one that Menuhin might have learned from concerts or records. From the very first violin entrance, it is clear that he has a fully formed idea of the solo part, and that he appreciates the difference in character between the orchestra's exposition of the themes and the violin's more raptly personal, even self-absorbed versions of them.

Nor can we assume that he absorbed this conception from Elgar, for there is a good deal of evidence to suggest that the composer usually played the concerto somewhat more tautly than he does here. A fascinating comparison, in fact, can be made between the Menuhin recording and a slightly earlier one by the English violinist Albert Sammons, conducted by Sir Henry J. Wood (UK: World Records SH-288), two interpreters whose work Elgar is known to have much admired. Sammons and Wood play the first movement in about fourteen-and-a-half minutes, while Menuhin and Elgar take more than seventeen—a considerable difference in a work of this length. In fact, both performances are perfectly convincing; Sammons/Wood does not seem rushed, while Menuhin/Elgar, though it takes its time, never drags. It seems likely that Elgar gladly accepted Menuhin's different way of playing the concerto, though his own tendencies as an interpreter of his works were rather different— an interesting sidelight on the question of authenticity discussed in the Introduction.

Menuhin's tone is sweet and full, his security even in the highest positions is uncanny, and his playing in the fast passages is fleet and powerfully shaped (like Brahms, Elgar builds his figurations from his thematic material). What Menuhin's Bach playing was like at that time can be tasted in the last movement when, in big, forceful multiple stops, he takes up the fast chorale theme previously stated by the orchestra. This last movement, formally unusual, is a sonata form with no development section, leading to an imaginative cadenza with orchestra accompaniment (including Elgar's "pizzicato tremolando," which requires the string players to thrum their instruments with the soft part of several fingers), recalling themes from previous movements, and drawing attention to their interrelationships.

Regrettably, Menuhin's early recordings are not now well represented in the catalogues (a collection of shorter pieces, US: Orion ORS-7271, should be avoided, since they are clumsily transferred from noisy source material), though a selection of his early concerto performances was available not long ago (UK: EMI/HMV RLS-

718, three disks). In his twenties Menuhin went through the first of several crises in his technique; since World War II, his playing has never quite recaptured the steadiness or the spontaneity of his early years. His thoughtfulness and idealism have remained notable, however, and his large catalogue of stereo recordings, though uneven in execution, includes most of the major works of the literature, especially the many 20th-century pieces that Menuhin has always vigorously espoused.

WILLIAM PRIMROSE
Viola

Berlioz: Harold in Italy, Op. 16 (with the Royal Philharmonic Orchestra, conducted by Sir Thomas Beecham; recorded 1951)

US: CBS Odyssey Y-33286

The viola serves sometimes as the alto voice, sometimes as the tenor, of the string family. Pitched a fifth lower than the violin, it produces a mellower, darker tone (although the quality of the highest string, the A string, tends to be somewhat nasal and penetrating). Physically larger than the violin, the viola has never been standardized in size, varying by as much as two inches in length. The reason for this is that the viola is an acoustical compromise; if it were truly proportionate in size to the violin, it would be half again as long and thus impossible to play at the shoulder; it would have to be set on the floor like a cello. So, over the centuries, various dimensions have been tried in the search for the best combination of tonal quality and playing convenience. (As with violins, most older instruments were altered during the 19th century, and are now played with 19th-century bows.)

The viola's technique is fundamentally similar to that of the violin, with allowances for its larger size that requires large hands and strong fingers. The stretches between notes on the strings are longer, and a greater bowing pressure is needed to set the thicker strings vibrating (thus the kind of delicate bowing effects so characteristic of the violin are more difficult on the viola). Many violists began as violinists, shifting to the lower instrument at some stage in their education or early ca-

William Primrose made a successful career as a solo violist, overcoming the instrument's traditional limitations of technique and repertoire.

reers, and some well-known violinists (Menuhin and Zukerman among them) have also made solo appearances as violists.

The most eminent violist of the middle part of the present century, William Primrose (b. 1903), was one who began as a violinist, studying in his native Glasgow and in London; the great Belgian violinist Ysaÿe turned him toward the viola. In the 1930s Primrose began a career as a soloist, also playing with the London String Quartet and, from 1937 to 1942, as principal violist with Toscanini's NBC Symphony. He continued to perform as soloist and chamber musician into the 1960s, and has been active as a teacher since his retirement.

The repertoire for viola solo and orchestra is not large, though Primrose has worked to augment it: the Viola Concerto that Bartók was working on at the time of his death, and which was completed by Tibor Serly, was a Primrose commission. The German composer Paul Hindemith was himself a violist and wrote a number of works. And there are extensive chamber-music opportunities for the violist (for example, Mozart's String Quintets, with two violas), although the best-known sonatas for the instrument, the two by Brahms, are in fact transcriptions of works originally (and very specifically) composed for clarinet.

The major 19th-century concerto for the viola is, in fact, not really a concerto: *Harold in Italy*, which the violinist Paganini commissioned from Berlioz after acquiring a Stradivarius viola, is really a symphonic poem with a prominent solo part. The viola represents Byron's Childe Harold—and Berlioz himself—as spectator of four genre scenes: a mountain landscape, a march of pilgrims, an Abruzzi mountaineer's serenade, and an orgy of brigands. Throughout, the viola sings the theme of Harold, which is set forth three times, in different instrumental garbs, in the slow introduction to the first movement. Although he sometimes joins in the other musical activity (as in the allegro of the first movement, when it proposes the principal theme), Harold's main role is as onlooker.

Among the striking passages in Berlioz's always inventive scoring is the *canto religioso* near the end of the "March of the Pilgrims," with viola arpeggios played *sul ponticello* (at the bridge), and the subsequent fading of the pilgrims' march crowned by a high harmonic note from the viola. In the "Serenade," the introduction, with drone bass and piping melodies, and the serenade itself, first sung by the English horn, are eventually combined. The last movement begins with recollections of themes from earlier movements, all of them rejected by the boisterous brigands; near the end, we hear the chant of the pilgrims once again (played by two violins and a cello, and joined by the solo viola), but even this does not forestall the noisy climax of the orgy.

Throughout, the poise and lyricism of Primrose's playing are admirable; though not full of conspicuously difficult passages (which is why Paganini never deigned to play the work he had commissioned), *Harold* is not easy, and you will not often hear it played with such security. Given the nature of the piece, the conductor has the determining role in the interpretation; here, in the second of Primrose's three recordings of *Harold*, it is Sir Thomas Beecham, a great Berliozian and equally a master of the fine orchestral detail and the rhythmic vivacity that figure so prominently in the composer's work.

Primrose's recording of the Bartók Viola Concerto (US: Bartók BRS-309) may be hard to find. Two other notable modern works, Hindemith's *Der Schwanendreher* and, Walton's Concerto, is likely to be more accessible (US: CBS Odyssey Y-35922), as also a recording of the Brahms Sonatas with Rudolf Firkusny (US: Seraphim 60011, stereo). Primrose's final recording of *Harold in Italy*, with Charles Munch, is recorded in stereo (US: RCA Gold Seal AGL1-1526), but is less well crafted than the Beecham version. Some chamber-music recordings will be mentioned below, in connection with Emanuel Feuermann.

PABLO CASALS
Cello

Dvořák: Cello Concerto in B minor, Op. 104 (with the Czech Philharmonic Orchestra, conducted by George Szell; recorded 1937)

US: Seraphim 60240; UK: EMI/HMV HLM-7013

The cello, pitched an octave lower than the viola, is sometimes the bass voice of the strings (especially in a string quartet) and sometimes, when its still larger relative the double bass is on hand, the tenor. Because it is held between the legs and supported on the ground by a peg, and because it is so much bigger than the violin and viola, many aspects of its technique are radically different. The left and rights hands still perform their traditional functions, but from quite different angles, while all the differences between violin and viola are magnified.

Not until the 20th century did the cello become a completely satisfactory solo instrument in its own right. The man who gave it that status was the Catalonian cellist Pablo Casals (1876-1973). There had been cello virtuosos before, and during the 19th century they adapted many of the showier techniques of violin playing to the cello, but its tonal quality still left much to be desired. Even Dvořák, who wrote what is universally regarded as the greatest concerto for the cello, complained about the "nasal quality" of its upper register and the "mumbling" of the lower notes. Only later did players come along who could do justice to Dvořák's work.

Casals began experimenting with the bowing and fingering of the instrument at the age of eleven. Two years later, in a music shop, he discovered the six Suites for unaccompanied cello of Johann Sebastian Bach—arcane works, long unplayed in their original form. For a dozen years, Casals worked at the technical challenges of Bach's music: getting his fingers and bow around the notes, the many fast passages, and the difficult chords, and making his tone lithe and warm to enliven the austere patterns, to shape them into music. Through this self-teaching, Casals made himself into the first modern cellist—and made the cello comparable to the violin in agility, intensity, and individuality of tonal color, an instrument with a personality rich and complex enough to sustain the soloist's spotlight.

Pablo Casals, the inventor of modern cello technique, one of the great interpreters, and in later years active as a teacher and conductor (here, at one of the Casals Festivals in the early 1950s).

Dvořák's Concerto is traditional enough to employ the Classical double exposition, and the orchestral presentation is so expansive that one begins to wonder whether a soloist will be needed at all. The first theme, terse, motto-like, builds to a grandiose climax; the second theme, a broad melody in the major, arrives in the horn. Both themes turn out to be admirably suited to the cello, which takes up the first in an improvisatory manner, asserting the instrument's rugged and forceful potential. Listen to Casals's very first note: the slashing rasp of the initial attack already defines character, and he keeps the dotted rhythms tight, pressing forward steadily. (For contrast, listen to a later performance by the same orchestra, with Mstislav Rostropovich as soloist: his tone is splendid but so leisurely in his schmoozy way with this passage as to fatally undermine the contrast between first and second subject; US: Quintessence PMC-7142.)

After an ascending chain of trills—Casals's tone firm and rich all the way up—the cello offers an ornamented version of the first subject, played with bounding vigor and precise articulation. When he takes up the second subject, it is with a tone comparable in warmth and richness to that of the horn, for which the melody had previously seemed so ideally suited; observe how cleanly the upward intervals are played, without sliding into the notes. In the slow movement, Casals has here and there simplified the writing, though without significantly altering the musical effect. Admirable here, as throughout, is the playing of the Czech orchestra, especially the winds (how sensitively they match phrasings with the cellist) and brass (such as the three horns that recapitulate the principal theme).

The temptation to luxuriate in Dvořák's melodies must be great, but surely needs resisting, for the composer has already indulged himself in that direction, especially in the coda to the final rondo, which spins ruminatively on, even dreamily recalling themes from the earlier movements. Casals and Szell firmly resist temptation; the way this performance keeps a move on is one of its great strengths. Above all, though, one retains in memory the vibrant cello tone, secure in intonation even in the highest register and the most difficult passagework, and the direct, natural musicality.

During the 1930s, Casals recorded much of the major cello literature. His famous interpretations of the Bach Suites for solo cello restored those works to the living repertoire (US: Angel 3786; UK: EMI/HMV RLS-712, three disks). His first recordings of the Beethoven sonatas, with Mieczyslaw Horszowski and (in No. 3) Otto Schulhof are magisterial (G: EMI/Electrola C-147-01538/9, two disks; US: Columbia M5-30069, Sonata No. 3 only, in a Casals retrospective collection; five disks). A good collection of his prewar recordings in solo, chamber, and concert works has been published in Britain, in first-class transfers (UK: EMI/HMV RLS-723, three disks). The selection of encore pieces includes a lightning traversal of Rimsky-Korsakov's *Flight of the Bumblebee*, that old violin showpiece, that leaves no doubt of Casals's power to make his instrument do anything a fiddle can.

After the defeat of the Loyalists in the Spanish Civil War, Casals settled in Prades, just across the border in France. In 1946, when he realized that the victorious Allies were not going to unseat the Fascist government in Spain, Casals cancelled all his engagements and retired from public appearances in protest. In 1950, at Prades, a series of festivals was inaugurated, whereby the world came to Casals; later, when he moved to Puerto Rico, the festivals were transferred there. In the postwar period, Casals's playing grew more mannered, but as soloist, conductor, and teacher, he remained a powerful influence. (His recordings of chamber music will be considered in the next section.)

5

CHAMBER MUSIC

*T*he term "chamber music" usually refers to music for small groups of solo instruments—from two to ten, as a rule—that is intended for performance in relatively small rooms rather than large concert halls. A narrower definition, proposed by the great musical analyst Sir Donald Tovey, calls attention to some central concerns: "music in large forms for a group of solo instruments on equivalent planes of tone and of equivalent musical capacity." The reference to "large forms" is presumably intended to exclude salon music and encore pieces. Another of the operative words here is "solo"; in chamber music there is only one player to a part. Implicit in Tovey's definition is another important consideration, that the group of musicians is not conducted; they maintain *ensemble*—that is, keep together—by mutual alertness and as a result of prior agreement and ample rehearsal, rather than by following the beat of a leader. In most modern ensembles, decisions about interpretation are also arrived at mutually, and the small size of the group and the nature of the music often encourage a greater degree of spontaneously inspired detail than would ever be practical in orchestral music-making. If one player should lay special stress on a note in a theme, the others will hear him and follow his example.

"Equivalent planes of tone" is Tovey's concise way of suggesting that although the string instruments and the piano are quite different in harmonic capability, dynamic range, and tonal characteristics, they can be made to work together with some accommodation from both sides. The pianist needs to keep the instrument's volume and weight of tone from overwhelming his colleagues, and the string players must remember that the pianist cannot "bend" pitches or phrase with the same kind of legato that they command. In writing for such combinations, of course, one point of interest is the different aspect that musical material assumes when played alternatively with sustaining string tone and with more percussive piano tone. (In Baroque music, the preferred keyboard instrument is the harpsichord; although the nature of the tonal contrast differs, the principle still holds.)

Standard Chamber Ensembles

Among the standard Classical-Romantic combinations with piano are the duo sonata (keyboard with one string or wind instrument), piano trio (piano, violin, cello), piano quartet (piano, violin, viola, cello), and piano quintet (piano, two violins, viola, and cello). Exceptional combinations have also been used to good effect: the most famous quintet for piano and strings is Schubert's "Trout," in which the strings are violin, viola, cello, and double bass.

Mention of the double bass brings attention back to Tovey's other criterion, "equivalent musical capacity." The behemoth of the string family may, under the hands of the finest modern virtuoso, be able to keep up with its smaller relatives, but that certainly was not the case in the 19th century, which is why it was rarely used in chamber music. Schubert's "Trout" Quintet works, in fact, because he does not ask the double bass to keep up but uses it principally as a foundation, achieving an almost *al fresco* sound for a particularly relaxed and informal work.

For this reason the string quartet, the most used of chamber-music combinations and the medium for the most exalted works, comprises not one each of the four different string instruments but a pair of violins, a viola, and a cello—all of which can function at pretty much an equivalent musical level, exchanging the same material and the same textural patterns with ease. This balance among the elements is one reason for the string quartet's eminence as a medium, from Haydn, Mozart, and Beethoven to Bartók, Schoenberg, and Carter in the present century. Paradoxically, another reason is its homogeneity of tone color; the lack of extreme timbral contrasts means that the composer must concentrate on abstract matters of melodic, harmonic, and rhythmic substance rather than exploiting the more obvious color contrasts that arise when strings are combined with piano or with a wind instrument.

Although there have been styles of writing in which the other three instruments were primarily reduced to the role of accompanying the first violinist, the Classical use of the string quartet medium is to treat it as a kind of four-voiced instrument with a range of over four octaves from which solo lines often emerge. In the course of the string quartet's evolution from the middle of the 18th century, a crucial point came with the introduction, by Haydn and then Mozart, of fugal textures that required all four instruments to engage in strict imitation of the same musical material. Another landmark is a group of quartets that Mozart composed for a cello-playing King of Prussia, which liberated that instrument from its traditional task of always carrying the bottom line of the texture. The viola, in the middle of the range, was less easily brought to prominence—although, as we shall see, Brahms found a way.

A texture more demanding of the composer is the string trio (violin, viola, and cello) because harmonic progressions are not as smoothly or as easily made in three parts as in four—a challenge notably met by both Mozart and Beethoven. The string quintet, on the other hand, yields an exceptionally rich texture, whether with two violas, which Mozart found particularly congenial, or with two cellos, as in Schubert's unique and transcendent Quintet in C major. The string sextet (two each of violin, viola, and cello) is even richer and darker, a color that was put to good use by both Brahms and Schoenberg. For the string octet (string quartet multiplied by two), there is one masterpiece, Mendelssohn's miracle of gossamer lightness. Quartets or quintets that combine strings with a single wind are common, but all-wind ensembles such as the wind quintet (flute, oboe, clarinet, horn, bassoon) tend to be less fluent and flexible, so their music has often been of a lighter character.

Amateurs and Professionals

To return again to our original definition: the setting, "small rooms rather than large concert halls," implies intimate, even domestic circumstances. Especially in the 18th century, much chamber music was played at home by amateurs of the middle class or the aristocracy. Professionals were also employed to play in private homes, and as a result composers eventually wrote music of a difficulty that excluded all but the finest amateurs. As the music became more demanding, it also tended to become more "public": the chamber music of Beethoven's middle period has a virtuosic element clearly implying an audience that is to be impressed rather than one that is simply eavesdropping on intimate music-making.

The most famous string quartet of the 19th century was that led by Joseph Joachim; though evidently more of a one-man show than later groups, it set new standards of ensemble and technical accomplishment (Joachim was fond of decorating the melodic line in Beethoven's slow movements, a practice that has since been regarded as undesirable). In the 20th century, there have been many celebrated quartets and some fairly stable piano trios and duo combinations. Celebrated soloists often join forces for chamber music, with varying results; the solo mentality is different from the attitude appropriate in a group, and not everyone can make the transition.

SZIGETI & BARTÓK
Violin & Piano

Beethoven: Violin Sonata No. 9, in A major, Op. 47 ("Kreutzer") • Debussy: Violin Sonata • Bartók: Violin Sonata No. 2; Rhapsody No. 1 (recorded at concert, 1940)
US: Vanguard SRV-304/5, two disks, electronic stereo

One of the 20th century's greatest composers, Béla Bartók (1881–1945) was also a remarkable pianist—and not only as an exponent of his own music. In 1905 he took second prize (to the renowned Wilhelm Backhaus) in the Prix Rubinstein piano competition, and he later toured extensively as a soloist. His teaching, too, concentrated on the piano; Bartók did not believe composition could be taught, but he was professor of piano at the Budapest Conservatory from 1907 until 1934. Our most important document of Bartók as a performer of major works is the fortunately preserved recording of a recital that he gave with his friend and compatriot Joseph Szigeti at the Library of Congress in Washington, D.C., in 1940, shortly before the composer settled permanently in the US.

In the 18th century, the duo sonata offered two alternative postures for the keyboard instrument. It could be strictly an accompaniment to its melodic partner—so much so that the details of its part were not actually written out but were merely suggested by a bass line with a shorthand indication of the harmonies (a system known as *basso continuo*). On the other hand, it could be the principal instrument, with the violin (or whatever) an optional partner whose omission would not in any way cripple the piece's musical substance. Gradually an equalization of the two partners came about, a give-and-

Béla Bartók and Joseph Szigeti, in Berlin, 1929; the collaboration of these great Hungarian musicians was resumed in a memorable 1940 recital in Washington, D.C.

take exploiting the strengths of both, although even in Beethoven's day many works that today are called violin sonatas were described on their title pages as "sonatas for piano and violin."

The equality is unquestionable in Beethoven's Sonata in A major, Op. 47, nicknamed the "Kreutzer" after the French virtuoso violinist to whom it is dedicated; to the title, Beethoven added the phrase, "written in a very *concertante* style, almost like a concerto." The violin begins alone, Adagio, with a broad phrase in multiple stops, to which the piano replies; their dialogue builds to the main body of the movement, a vigorous Presto that is punctuated at crucial junctures with long-held chords. The stride of this movement depends on a vivid articulation of the staccato principal subject, on a precise observation of the many strong accents (often syncopated), and on maintaining a sweep of momentum and tension even through those long-held chords. The intensity and concentration that Szigeti and Bartók achieve in their performance is simply overwhelming.

The slow movement is a set of variations, on a theme in which Bartók's practice of rolling chords may be initially distracting. (Surprisingly, this habit does not detract from the impetus of the first movement at all, demonstrating that it need not—though it often does—create a sloppy effect.) The shape of Beethoven's theme is AA BABA; he writes it out in full the first time, but in the first three variations uses repeat signs to indicate that A, and then BA, should be repeated; in the fourth, most florid variation, the repetitions are written out because they are themselves varied. By omitting the repetitions in the first three variations, Szigeti and Bartók rather shortchange the overall proportions of the movement, but we can only treasure the playing, especially Bartók's softly crystalline trills and other ornamentation in the fourth variation, which suggest what his playing of a late Beethoven piano sonata must have been like.

The tarantella whirl of the final rondo is, like the drive of the first movement, occasionally relieved by brief relaxations; once again, the energy level is amazing, the specificity of the phrasing and accenting memorable. Four years later, also at the Library of Congress, Szigeti played the ten Beethoven Sonatas with the Chilean pianist Claudio Arrau, but that "Kreutzer" is both a much less vividly inflected performance, and a fascinating demonstration of how different partners can affect the playing of even the finest musician (US: Vanguard SRV-300/303, four disks, electronic stereo).

The Violin Sonata that was Claude Debussy's last completed work is a very different matter. Though its first movement is marked Allegro vivo, any such pace of activity is at first clouded in ambiguity, and the vigorous three-beat motion achieved at the first climax fades away several times. Rhythmic ambiguity is a central feature of the music, and so is a bias in the harmony that makes the final chords of all three movements seem less than definitive. The Bartók/Szigeti performance, vigorous and muscular, certainly does not conform to any Gallic tradition as is heard, say, in the recording of Thibaud and Cortot (and, in truth, it is often a degree or two louder than Debussy's dynamic markings), but it is consistently absorbing.

Bartók's two violin sonatas are among his most dissonant and impressive works. The Second Sonata, in two movements, is an expansion of the traditional Hungarian pattern—exemplified also in the First Rhapsody, included in this concert—of a rhapsodic slow introduction and a fast, dancelike conclusion. Much of the music has an irregular, improvisatory character, playing freely with tempo and meter. The first movement begins with a sustained, decaying note in the piano's low register that is answered by a much higher note from the violin, also fading away on repetition; the principal theme then follows from the violin. Several times in the movement that same violin note recurs, each time leading to a fresh expansion before the main theme returns at the end. (In the last expansion, the violin replaces its usual sustained single notes with grating double stops.) Bartók calls for a considerable range of exotic effects from the violin, such as harmonics and glissandos, all vividly realized by Szigeti; and the same intensity that sustains the ''Kreutzer'' Sonata is essential to maintain the tension of this elastic movement.

The irregular dance theme of the second movement is first presented in violin pizzicatos, and a contrasting tune in the piano is accompanied by rough, percussive repeated notes on the violin. That basic theme, involving upward and then downward motion, is not unrelated to the main theme of the first movement, whose double stops return briefly at one point, following a more relaxed section in which Bartók accompanies the violin's slow line with a very free treatment of what he wrote as chords of even length. Eventually the violin, muted at first, resumes the principal dance theme in a dizzy whirl of not-quite-perpetual motion, which eventually exhausts itself into a calm recall of the first movement's theme and closing mood. The tricky cross-rhythms between the instruments, the irregular meters and phrases, are played with commanding poise and powerful energy. Despite the occasional ill effects of Bartók's rolled chords, this performance—like that of the slighter Rhapsody—is much more than a document; it is an indelible musical experience.

For all that, one may well find Bartók's recordings of other people's music even more revelatory of his mind and spirit. This is not entirely paradoxical; when playing his own works, he gives us aspects of himself about which the music has already told us a good deal, while the music of Beethoven and Debussy summons up unfamiliar facets of his personality. Alas, there are few additional recorded examples of Bartók playing other composers: a dim broadcast from 1929 preserves four Scarlatti sonatas, lucid and subtly accented, and there is a studio recording of a late Liszt piece, *Sursum corda* (US:

Bartók 903, which also contains a number of shorter Bartók works; the dubbings are somewhat pallid).

Of Bartók playing Bartók, there is rather more, and as of this writing all his recordings for English and Hungarian EMI during the late 1920s and 1930s are scheduled for release by Hungaroton, a label well distributed in the US and UK. These are vivid performances, especially a large selection of folksong arrangements by Bartók and his colleague Kodály, earthily sung by members of the Budapest Opera of fifty years ago. (Two groups of short pieces arranged for violin and piano, played with Szigeti, are included in the big Szigeti set discussed earlier as well as in the Hungarian set.) In the US, Bartók recorded his *Contrasts*, written for Benny Goodman and Szigeti, and also a substantial selection from *Mikrokosmos*, his marvelous graded anthology of pieces for young pianists (US: CBS Odyssey 32-16-0220, electronic stereo; UK: CBS 61882; a further selection of *Mikrokosmos* pieces is currently unavailable). Some other short pieces are collected on US: Turnabout THS-65010.

Szigeti recorded much chamber music with a variety of partners, although most of it comes from later years when his tone was less alluring and his techniques less reliable than before. In addition to the already-mentioned set of Beethoven Sonatas from concerts with Arrau, two Beethoven Sonatas from a New York recital with Schnabel are included in the big Szigeti set—roughly recorded but quite grandly played. In a prewar recording not currently available, Szigeti collaborated with the great Dutch pianist Egon Petri in the Brahms Third Sontas in D minor. An example of his advocacy of contemporary music is the Ives Violin Sonata No. 4, recorded in 1942 for American avant-garde composer Henry Cowell's New Music Quarterly label (US: Composers Recordings CRI-390, electronic stereo, with other early recordings of Ives's music). Among his later chamber music recordings, two sets of Mozart Sonatas with Mieczyslaw Horszowski and George Szell are still in the catalogues (US: Vanguard SRV-262/4 and SRV-265/7, three disks each, electronic stereo); these and many other recordings from the 1940s and 1950s are never without musical interest, despite their occasional technical deficiencies. The later Mercury disks—all now out of print—are less dependable still, though they are better recorded.

FEUERMANN & HESS
Cello & Piano

Beethoven: Cello Sonata No. 3 in A major, Op. 69 (recorded
1937) • Schubert: Sonata in A minor for Arpeggione and Piano (Feuermann
with Gerald Moore; recorded 1937) • Weber: Andantino and Variations
(Feuermann with Moore; recorded 1936)
US: Seraphim 60117

The great cellist of the generation after Casals was the
Austrian Emanuel Feuermann (1902–1942), whose career was tragically cut short at its height when he died in
a New York hospital of complications following a minor
operation. While Feuermann still lived, the Spanish cellist acknowledged the younger man's instrumental mastery; Casals could hardly have imagined that, having
first played in public before Feuermann was born, he
would still be playing two decades after his death. Before
he was twenty, Feuermann was appointed to the faculty
of the Leipzig Conservatory; later he taught in Berlin,
and joined the faculty of the Curtis Institute when he
came to the US in 1938.

The British pianist Myra Hess (1890–1965) never won a
virtuoso's following, but her solid, unspectacular musicianship was always greatly admired in Britain and
America. Frequently active in chamber music, during
World War II she founded and organized the famous
midday concerts in London's National Gallery. Apparently she and Feuermann had not worked together before their recording of the Beethoven A major Cello
Sonata, but their collaboration is remarkably harmo-
nious and integrated.

The cello begins the Sonata alone, with the first limb of
a theme, to which the piano replies—and then makes a
cadenza before taking its turn at the beginning of the
theme. This time the cello takes over the reply and makes
its own cadenza. In these two statements, Beethoven has
set forth significant contrasts of register, tone color, and
musical potential (for example, the cello's single-line
opening as opposed to the piano's presentation of the
same phrase doubled over four octaves). A vigorous syncopated transition, which clearly derives its shape from
the first theme, leads to the new key and a theme in the
piano whose rhythm is basically identical with that of the

Emanuel Feuermann, the extraordinary cellist whose career was cut tragically short just as he was achieving full international recognition.

first theme. Nor is Beethoven's thematic integration finished here, for an additional theme, first in the piano and then in the lower reaches of the cello, builds on the dotted rhythm and trill from the end of the first theme!

The development concentrates on a pathetic descending variant of this related material, and the recapitulation, heralded by intimations of the original theme, is confided to the cello, this time under a filigree of piano rather than alone. This spacious movement, with its many open sonorities (allowing the cello comfortably to penetrate the piano's textures), never goes slack at the hands of Feuermann and Hess, who play with energy and much rhythmic force and profile. The cello tone is extraordinarily warm and rich, never overripe, always fluent and flexible.

One of Beethoven's middle-period strategies for increasing the substance of his inner movements was to amplify the usual pattern of Scherzo and Trio by an additional repetition: thus, ABABA instead of a simple ABA. In this Sonata, he actually wrote out all the repetitions—but, alas, presumably to fit the side-length limitations of 78 RPM records, Feuermann and Hess have cut it back to ABA. The wonderful straining-at-the-bit syncopations are played with invigorating poise and spring. This is followed by a brief slow movement—more of an interlude, really—in which the cello takes first an inner voice and then the melody. Although showier, the final Allegro re-

Dame Myra Hess, the much-loved British pianist and chamber musician, whose perfectionism was such that she only infrequently made recordings.

captures much of the openness of the first movement (the relation between their themes is not hard to detect), and it is played with dash and impeccable technique, especially the many fast cello scales, in which every note is perfectly true and clear, nothing smudged.

In the other two works on this disk, Feuermann collaborates with Gerald Moore, (b. 1899), a British pianist whose greatest fame came from his work as the preferred accompanist of many celebrated *Lieder* singers such as Elisabeth Schwarzkopf and Dietrich Fischer-Dieskau; Moore has probably recorded more song accompaniments than any pianist in history.

The arpeggione was a short-lived instrument of the early 19th century, essentially a kind of bass viol; though tuned like a guitar and equipped with frets, it was bowed like a cello. This curious hybrid is remembered today solely because Franz Schubert wrote for it a far-from-inconsequential work. His Arpeggione Sonata has been adopted, not only by cellists, but—to judge from current recordings—also by clarinetists and double-bass players; for that matter, thanks to the original-instrument movement, there is now even a recording on the arpeggione!

Even with considerable adaptation to fit the range of the cello, the Arpeggione Sonata is a major technical challenge; more of a melody-instrument-with-accompaniment piece than, say, the Beethoven A major Sonata, it also gives the cellist little respite. The melancholy lyricism of the opening is set off by a bustling second subject with many upward leaps, which Feuermann accomplishes with great security; note, too, how carefully he follows Schubert's articulation of this theme, legato when it first appears, then on repetition alternating legato and staccato.

The songful slow movement implies a ternary (ABA) form, but although the home key returns, the original theme never does, and the cello leads into the amiable final movement, whose two principal themes clearly proclaim their ties with the corresponding themes of the first movement. (Beethoven was not the only composer concerned with thematic integration!). Though Feuermann and Moore take the important repetitions when the various themes are introduced and thus maintain the music's basic proportions, they are forced to make some cuts of repeated material later on—but that is the only flaw in this wonderful performance, at once genial and utterly concentrated. The amiable Weber Variations, arranged from a showpiece for cello and orchestra, emerge as something almost profound in Feuermann's hands.

There are, alas, too few Feuermann recordings, and too few of those are available. With the Philadelphia Orchestra, he recorded a fervent performance of Bloch's *Schelomo* conducted by Stokowski, and a noble, imaginative one of Strauss's *Don Quixote* conducted by Ormandy; deplorably, both have been out of print for years. The Brahms Double Concerto, conducted by Ormandy, is in one of the RCA Heifetz sets (US: RCA Red Seal ARM4-0945), and a lower-priced recital disk is also still listed (US: RCA Victrola VIC-1476). The latter contains some recordings published only after Feuermann's death and possibly against his wishes—there is a patch of poor intonation near the end of the second movement of Mendelssohn's Sonata in D major, and the rest of the music is not heavyweight.

Earlier, in Europe, Feuermann recorded the Haydn Concerto in D major, as well as string trios with Szymon Goldberg and Paul Hindemith, Brahms's First Cello Sonata, and a Suite for Solo Cello by Max Reger, but these and other British Columbia items are not now available. In the US, he took part in a highly publicized series of chamber-music recordings with Jascha Heifetz and Artur Rubinstein. Although the cello playing is unfailingly magnificent, those performances have never seemed entirely satisfactory; somehow the energy that is audible on the records remains independent of the music itself. The repertoire included the same Beethoven and Schubert trios that Cortot, Thibaud, and Casals had recorded, plus the Brahms Trio No. 1 in B major (US: RCA Red Seal LM-7025, two disks). In fact, the most successful products of this series of sessions was a string trio, Dohnányi's Serenade in C major, in which Heifetz and Feuermann were joined by Primrose (US: RCA Red Seal LVT-1017); the same group recorded Mozart's masterpiece for string trio, the Divertimento in E-flat major, K. 563 (US: RCA Red Seal CRM-2264; UK: RCA RL-42474, six disks—the Heifetz chamber-music collection). There is some broadcast material, as well as a very early recording of the Dvořák Concerto, which suffers from scrappy orchestral playing and poor recording, but the current underground editions of these and the British Columbia recordings are not too satisfactory.

Surprisingly, none of Myra Hess's recordings are now available in her native land, but the US catalogues list her warmly affectionate performances of Schumann's Piano Concerto and Symphonic Etudes (Seraphim 60009).

CORTOT, THIBAUD & CASALS
Piano, Violin & Cello

Beethoven: Trio in B-flat major, Op. 97 ("Archduke"), for Piano, Violin and Cello (recorded 1928) • Variations in G, Op. 121a (recorded 1926)
US: **Seraphim 60242;** *UK*: **World Records SH-230**

Before World War I, Alfred Cortot and Pablo Casals formed a piano trio with the French violinist Jacques Thibaud (1880–1953), who had been a pupil of the Belgian virtuoso Marsick at the Paris Conservatory, where he took first prize in 1896. The trio endured until the 1930s, and in the early days of electrical recording they made a group of recordings that quickly became famous, for they show an exceptionally successful collaboration among celebrated soloists, who had played together so often that their personal idiosyncrasies had become attuned to a greater whole.

Beethoven's Trio in B-flat major, Op. 97 (known as the "Archduke" because it is dedicated to the composer's patron Archduke Rudolph of Austria) is one of his most spacious works, not only because of the expansiveness of its principal themes and the generally moderate tempos but also because of the breadth of its modula-

Pablo Casals, Alfred Cortot, and Jacques Thibaud, three exceptional soloists who joined forces to make an equally notable chamber ensemble.

tions. In the first movement the grand opening theme is given first by the piano and then by the violin. (In between these two statements the strings make a little cadenza; observe the mannerly give and take between Thibaud and Casals as they defer to each other's phrase and then match tones in duet.) Then comes a fairly abrupt modulation leading to an unusually "bright" key for the second group—in fact, a step higher than the expected dominant.

The development reverts to more expectable regions, dealing in turn with various segments of the first theme: its first five notes, then only the second, third, and fourth notes, and then moving on to the next limb, the ascending phrase. A remarkable passage ensues, with pizzicato strings, trills, and staccato diminutions of that phrase, all brilliantly and precisely realized in this performance; the accumulated tension is suddenly diverted by fresh attention to the beginning of the theme—and then some trills dissolve into a soft, slightly ornamented recapitulation, this time in normal harmonic regions.

Another aspect of the spaciousness of the "Archduke" is the scale of the Scherzo; like that of the Cello Sonata in A, it is given extra weight by an extra repetition of Trio and Scherzo—and then still more, for the crabbedly chromatic and imitative Trio starts up once again—only to be quickly cut short. Unfortunately, as in the Feuermann/Hess recording of Op. 69, the extra repetition has been omitted here. The principal theme, a Beethovenian ingenuity distilled from a simple scale, is articulated with wit and bounce by these players, and Cortot's *panache* in the surprising waltz that several times crashes into the Trio is particularly delightful.

The slow movement is a set of variations, on a theme in two parts; the first half is always repeated in its entirety (in a different instrumental guise), but only the last four measures of the second half are so restated. This theme does not modulate from the home key of D major nor even briefly venture any distance (in that respect, it is even more static than the slow movement of the Violin Concerto). In each of the first four variations the unit of motion becomes smaller, and the fourth variation is marked "a little slower" to accomodate the very small subdivisions of the beat that result. The fifth variation returns to the beginning, but turns out to be a new harmonization, heading in mysterious directions (particularly beautiful is Thibaud's hesitation on the last note of his phrase, which unexpectedly brings the melody back home). The second phrase gets stuck, stutters, and then ascends to a step above its normal climax. From this distance, a dreamlike coda gradually comes back down to earth with fragments of the theme; before the tonic has faded completely away, a foreign chord intervenes, preparing the finale. This Andante is raptly played by Cortot, Thibaud, and Casals, especially in the long-drawn-out coda; Cortot's use of rolled chords for emphasis is very effective in the theme (as, indeed, it was at the beginning of the first movement).

The curious principal theme of the rondo finale, which ascends towards the wrong key and only homes in on B-flat when it turns downward, is very catchily played by Cortot, who also deftly teases the tempo in the second strain. When the first episode has returned a second time, preparations for yet another return of the principal theme are mysteriously diverted into another of those unexpectedly bright keys that Beethoven favors in this piece, and the expected theme appears in more or less the guise of a tarantella, over a long trill in the piano, which then returns to the point where this digression began. This time, we land in the home key, but still in the tarantella rhythm, in which an exuberant coda is made.

The filler to the "Archduke" is a set of variations for string trio, in which Beethoven conjures both remarkable profundity and jovial wit from an innocent operetta tune; the very solemn introduction is at once a joke (it raises our expectations too high for the simple theme) and entirely serious (suitable solemnities are eventually in store). For some reason, the Cortot/Thibaud/Casals recording of this piece was never issued on 78 RPM records;

the source material, which is marred by some surface grating, sounds like a set of test pressings, but the transfer has been admirably managed by EMI's Anthony Griffiths.

In addition to the "Archduke," Cortot, Thibaud, and Casals recorded Haydn's Trio No. 25 in G major and Schubert's Trio No. 1 in B-flat major (G: EMI/Electrola C-047-01148; F: EMI/Pathé-Marconi C-061-01148), Mendelssohn's Trio No. 1 in D minor and Schumann's Trio No. 1 in the same key (UK: EMI/HMV RLS-723, three disks, a Casals collection; G & F: EMI C-049-01808). Of these, the Schubert is the most famous, but all are fine examples of this collaboration. Another eloquent souvenir is a performance of the Brahms Double Concerto for Violin and Cello, played by Thibaud and Casals with the latter's Barcelona orchestra conducted by Cortot (UK: EMI/HMV RLS-723, the Casals collection again). Thibaud and Cortot also collaborated frequently, especially in the French literature—for example, the Chausson Concerto in D for Violin, Piano, and String Quartet (F: EMI/Pathé-Marconi C-051-03719), and sonatas by Debussy, Fauré, and Franck.

After World War II, at the Casals Festivals in Prades and Perpignan, the cellist took part in a number of chamber-music recordings. The most famous of these is his collaboration with Isaac Stern, Alexander Schneider, Milton Katims, and Paul Tortelier in Schubert's great Quintet in C major (US: CBS Columbia M5-30069, five disks, a Casals anthology; UK & G: CBS 61043). A set from Prades and Perpignan includes both chamber works and concertos conducted by Casals (US: CBS Columbia M5X-32768, five disks).

BUDAPEST QUARTET
String Quartet

"THE EARLY EMI RECORDINGS (1932/36)"

Mozart: Quartet No. 20 in D major, K. 499 • Beethoven: Quartet No. 8 in E minor, Op. 59, No. 2 • Quartet No. 13 in B-flat major, Op. 130 • Schubert: Quartet Movement in C minor, D. 703 • Mendelssohn: Quartet in E-flat major, Op. 12 • Brahms: Quartet No. 3 in B-flat major, Op. 67 • Wolf: Italian Serenade in G major • Bartók: Quartet No. 2, Op. 17. (recorded 1932-36)

US : CBS Odyssey Y4-34643, four disks

The best-known string quartet of the 20th century was founded in 1918 by four members of the orchestra at the Budapest Opera. By 1927, the second violinist had been twice replaced and was now a Russian, Joseph Roisman. In 1930 the original cellist was replaced by another Russian, Mischa Schneider, and in 1932 Emil Hauser, the leader, left to pursue a solo career. This brought about a major realignment, with Roisman moving up to first violin and Schneider's younger brother Alexander coming aboard as second. (At this time, Roisman purchased Hauser's Guarneri, so the same instrument remained in the lead throughout the Budapest's history). With this personnel—violist Istvan Ipolyi was the sole remaining Hungarian—the Budapest Quartet made the recordings under consideration here.

By all accounts the changeover from Hungarians to Russians made a significant difference in the Budapest sound (their earliest recordings are rather rare, and none have so far been transferred to LP). Roisman, especially, brought a more modern style of string playing, with more intense vibrato, tauter rhythm, and cleaner phrasing. The Budapest of these vintage years was the Rolls-Royce of string quartets, smooth and silken in tone, alert in ensemble, light and brilliant in staccato, secure in intonation. Mechanically, they were almost perfect, not only in the obvious sense of their management of the individual instruments and their unity and unanimity but also in the management of the total string-quartet texture. They knew how to make lines and chords balance so that the logic of the music's progression was not obscured, which is more than a simple matter of adjusting relative loudness; it also entails coordinating types of attack, carefully planning the swell and decay of individual notes, attending at all times to the total sound. The Budapest really presented the image of a unified instrument, the four individualities subordinated to an ideal of ensemble perfection.

This particular focus tends to create smooth performances rather than profound ones. The first three movements of Mozart's Quartet in D major, K. 499, straightforward in form and elegant in detail, are here nicely realized, with characteristically vivid pointing of the staccato accompaniment pattern that arises at the end of the first-movement exposition, and perfect matching of Mozart's frequent pairings and repairings of instruments. But the fourth movement, which takes a

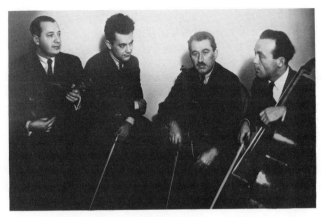

The Budapest Quartet of the early 1930s (l. to r., Joseph Roisman, Alexander Schneider, Istvan Ipolyi, and Mischa Schneider), the most famous string quartet of modern times.

while to locate its home key and remains interestingly off-center thereafter, comes out simply bland; its oddity is overlooked rather than explored.

The second of Beethoven's three "Razumovsky" Quartets (another nickname derived from a dedication) is a much bigger, more restless piece. It is also much more difficult to play than the Mozart; the first violin has to spend a good deal of time at an altitude that Mozart only rarely touches, and the writing is often florid, often rhythmically irregular. Implicit in a piece such as this was the need for professional string quartets.

The opening is arresting: a questioning pair of chords, a pause, an expansion of the chords into a terse, almost fugitive theme, another pause, then the theme, mysteriously, a half-step higher than before (a harmonic relation that will pervade the piece). Eventually some continuity is established, but the rhythm remains perversely restless, eventually dissolving from the original two strong beats (each subdivided in three) per measure to three syncopated ones.

Possibly for the usual problems with recording time the indicated repeats in this movement are not made— although the Budapest's LP version also omits them. This is a disappointment, for in this case Beethoven makes particularly dramatic use of this convention. Only if we have heard how he gets from the end of the exposition back to the beginning of the movement does the turn of events at the start of the development—those opening chords displaced harmonically—sound as startling as it should. And the same kind of thing happens at the end of the recapitulation, when the composer asks for an unusual repeat back to the beginning of the development; this he hardly ever gets, even today. The coda begins calmly, but the movement's tensions have clearly not been exorcised; it ends with a collapse rather than a resolution.

The bristling difficulties of this first movement are handsomely mastered by the Budapest. They also sustain the very long, very slow second movement—a vision of a different world—and set forth the third movement's nervous syncopations with perfect poise; in the Trio, built on a Russian theme that opera-goers will recognize from Mussorgsky's *Boris Godunov*, the bite of the two violins in the top register is exhilarating. Another of Beethoven's three-times-around Scherzos, this one, too, had to be truncated to fit the time limitations.

The Finale begins confidently in a "wrong" (and major) key, with a cheerfully naive theme that seems merely silly until it turns to the minor and the right key. Much of the movement makes play with the fact that the shortest way to get home to E minor is not via its normal preparation (its dominant, B major), but by setting up the dominant of the "wrong" key of C major in which the main theme begins; then, simply playing that theme will inevitably lead to E minor! Again, the playing is superb, the often-repeated dotted rhythm never flagging or growing sloppy, the vigorous contrapuntal episodes sharply limned and justly balanced.

To appreciate fully the impact of the Budapest performances of the 1930s, they ought to be compared with the works of contemporaries such as the Léner Quartet, whose resources did not include the kind of vigorous attacks or even the security of intonation, that, we hear in this recording. But the Budapest was not always so successful with Beethoven; in the B-flat Quartet, Op. 130, the rich tone and rather unvaried accenting weighs down a piece that clearly aims at a wide range of textural and formal contrasts. (Op. 130 originally ended with an enormous fugal movement, but Beethoven succumbed to the protests of his publisher and sustituted a lighter and easier piece, publishing the original finale separately as the *Great Fugue*. This change of ultimate destination is one of the problems with this ambitious and difficult work.) Rather than devoting space to a detailed analysis, I encourage comparison with the Busch Quartet's recording (see below), a stimulating and illuminating exercise.

We do not know what prevented Schubert from completing the String Quartet in C minor that he began in 1820; he broke it off after getting forty-one measures into the second movement. The splendid opening Allegro, now known as the Quartet movement (*Quartettsatz*, in German), begins and ends with a fierce wind, which blows up between the lyrical themes as well. The Budapest performances is taut and effective in holding together Schubert's extreme contrasts. (For once there was room on the record for an exposition repeat!)

Mendelssohn's First String Quartet shows in its formal arrangements that the twenty-year-old composer was a student of Beethoven's late sonatas and quartets; material from the first movement recurs in the finale, eventually bringing this stormy piece home from C minor to the repose of E-flat major. The content is not Beethovenian, however—especially the Canzonetta that stands in for a Scherzo. Here the Budapest players show off the elegance of their bouncing bows and the perfection of their ensemble in rapid passagework, and the whole performance is aptly ardent and propulsive. One flaw: the transfer engineer apparently did not know that the last movement must follow the third without a pause, and there is a disconcerting hiatus.

Among the best of these performances is certainly that of Brahms's Quartet No. 3 in B-flat major, Op. 67, a work full of complex and fascinating details that benefit greatly from the Budapest's clarity and security. Brahms plays a good deal with meter: the triply-subdivided duple meter of the opening horn calls is soon contested by assertions of triple time, the second subject subdivides the duple meter into twos, and two-against-three combinations are not rare. He plays with rhythm: the horn-call figure is variously accented. He plays with phrases; the regular ones that begin the slow movement eventually give way to less even ones, and in the middle section some extra beats creep in. He plays with instrumentation: the third movement is a masterpiece of scoring, in which the lead is given to the viola while the other instruments (all three muted) are relegated primarily to accompaniment; note particularly the beginning of the Trio, when the violins and cello play a phrase that sounds complete in itself—and then on repetition the viola supplies the melody to which the rest is in fact an accompaniment!

The last movement is a *tour de force* of another kind, a set of variations on an odd little theme, which appears to be ternary with repeats (AA BABA)—except that it is rounded off, not by the whole first phrase, but only by its first half. This irregularity is faithfully preserved in the variations, but nothing quite prepares for the extraordinary moment when, after the variations have led to a distant key, a sudden flourish brings back the horn-call theme of the first movement! This—to the enormous delight of Brahms, the Budapest Quartet, and the listener—quickly turns out to fit, with the slightest adjustments, into the pattern of these variations. Now, with triple subdivisions of the basic two-beat meter as well as the prior duple ones, Brahms can play at his favorite game again; the remaining variations and the coda bring about a gentle reconciliation of the work's various elements.

Equally susceptible to the Budapest's virtuosity is the brief, quicksilver *Italian Serenade*, one of Hugo Wolf's few instrumental pieces. The serenade is sung initially by the first violin, but the others take part in further developments, and there are amusing interruptions that suggest amorous altercations. Roisman balances the catchy rhythms of his tune deftly, on the tip of his bow.

Bartók's six quartets are generally recognized as the most significant contributions to the medium since Beethoven. The first recording ever made of his Second Quartet was the Budapest's—a competent piece of playing that does not, however, make much contact with the novel rhythmic or coloristic aspects of the work. Sadly, we have no recordings of the Waldbauer Quartet, to whom the Second Quartet is dedicated, and who introduced much of Bartók's chamber music; not until after World War II, when the then-new Juilliard Quartet took them up, did the Bartók Quartets achieve truly fitting performances on records.

Aside from the lapse in the Mendelssohn mentioned above, the transfers in Odyssey's Budapest Quartet's anthology are adequate, but no more. Transfers of these same recordings by EMI engineer Anthony Griffith have been released in Japan, but for some reason they did not please the CBS producer and new dubbings were made. I haven't heard the Griffith versions, but his transfers of the Busch Quartet recordings, made in the same studios during the same years as these Budapest sets, have more color and life in the string tone. A second set of prewar Budapest recordings (US: Odyssey Y3-35240, three disks) contains additional quartets by Mozart (K. 458, K.

465, K. 590) and Beethoven (Op. 18, Nos. 2 and 3, and Op. 74); on the cover is a picture of the city of Budapest (hardly relevant by this time), and two pictures of the Quartet, one of them showing a much later conformation that is not heard on these records. One Griffith transfer, the Budapest's excellent performance of the Sibelius Quartet, has been published in the West (World Records SH-285).

In 1936, the violist Ipolyi left the Quartet; his replacement, Boris Kroyt, made it an all-Russian group. In 1944, Alexander Schneider struck off on his own. Many of the recordings from these years have been reissued on CBS Odyssey, but they are played with less conviction and polish. Schneider returned in 1955, after the death of his second replacement, and by the time of the Budapest's stereo remakes (mostly still in the American catalogues), there was more life in the performances, but Roisman's tone and intonation had begun to deteriorate noticeably. Since the Budapest's greatest strengths were those of execution rather than interpretation, it is the sables-and-diamonds ensemble of the 1930s that is most rewarding to revisit.

BUSCH QUARTET
String Quartet

Beethoven: Quartet No. 12 in E-flat major, Op. 127 (recorded 1936) • Quartet No. 14 in C-sharp minor, Op. 131 (recorded 1936) • Quartet No. 16 in F major, Op. 135 (recorded 1936)

UK: World Records SHB-38, two disks; G: EMI/Electrola 1C-147-01668/70, three disks (with Quartet No. 15 in A minor, Op. 132)

Adolf Busch (1891-1952), whom we have already encountered in connection with Marcel Moÿse, was most celebrated as leader of the string quartet that bore his name. Busch came from a very musical family; he began to study the violin with his father at age three, entered the Cologne Conservatory at age eleven, and by 1912 was concertmaster of the Vienna Konzertverein Orchestra. At that time he founded the Vienna Konzertverein Quartet, which was disbanded during World War I, but in 1918 he reorganized it as the Busch Quartet. From 1921 on, the other members were Busch's student Gösta An-

The Busch Quartet (l. to r., Adolf Busch, Gösta Andreasson, Hermann Busch, and Paul Doktor), leading exponents of the German string quartet literature between the wars.

dreasson, the violist Paul Doktor, and the cellist Paul Grümmer, in 1931, Grümmer was replaced by Busch's younger brother, Hermann. After 1927, Busch made his headquarters in Basel and later became a Swiss citizen, but the members of the Quartet—and Busch's son-in-law Rudolf Serkin—moved to the US in 1939-40. The Quartet was disbanded in 1945, but the Busch brothers started again in 1946 with new colleagues; this later ensemble never acheived the high standards of the pre-World War II group.

The Busch Quartet's most celebrated achievements were its performances of Beethoven, especially the works of the late period, the composer's most personal and concentrated exploration of new formal and expressive possibilities in the sonata cycle. So novel were these pieces, and so complex of execution, that they were for many years played only rarely. Appreciation came slowly in the later 19th century, and has become universal in the 20th. More than simply the high point of the quartet literature, the late Beethoven quartets are often regarded as the most rarified and exalted achievements of the art of music, on both formal and spiritual planes.

The first of the group, Op. 127, is on the face of it quite ordinary: four movements, in the usual forms. But in fact they aren't at all usual. The first is an exceptionally lyrical sonata form, despite those imposingly full chords that start it off and recur at crucial junctures in the development. But they don't come back to make a drama of the recapitulation, which enters unheralded.

The slow movement is a set of variations on a very long-breathed theme. Though the theme is eminently lyrical, the course of the variations becomes dramatic. Right away, the theme is treated freely, unfolded in elaborate and fantastical textures. In the third variation, it is wrenched away from the home key of A-flat, only to return in the next. The tension rises again in the fifth variation, a mysterious piece in minor, and relaxes again in the sixth, the most fluent of all. The theme's little cadential tag is often present in the variations, and in the coda is transformed into a microcosm of the earlier harmonic crux.

Pizzicato chords introduce the Scherzo, which begins in orderly if somewhat learned fashion with its theme imitated in inversion (upside down). Eventually an extraordinary series of disruptions ensues, making the movement a startlingly aggressive sequel to two basically songful, euphonious pieces. The Trio, starting with a spooky fast passage, turns into a vigorous dance. After the repetition of the Scherzo, the Trio starts again—but this time the reprise is abruptly called off.

At the head of the Finale, there is no tempo marking. The principal theme, after an off-key start, suggests a certain asymmetry (3 + 5 measures rather than the normal 4 + 4), but the rest of the material is quite pointedly regular, often dancelike. Near the end, at the point where we anticipate a coda, there is a sudden harmonic shift and trills break out, leading to a new texture of luminous embroidery, surrounding what we soon realize is the main theme, only slightly disguised.

The Busch Quartet's performance of Op. 127 is remarkable in several ways. Rhythmic detail is always precise (as in the dotted rhythms of the Scherzo), and so is articulation—the spiky sound of the leader's staccato, so different from the bounced-bow type that the Budapest Quartet favors, soon becomes familiar. Portamento is used more often than is common today, but always aptly and thoughtfully. The lucidity of the performance owes much to the mastery of larger rhythmic matters. For example, the very slow quadruple meter of the Adagio can become submerged by an emphasis on the triple subdivisions of each beat (thus making a piece of four times as many metrical units), but Busch never lets that happen. And there is the gusto with which the group addresses Beethoven's accents, and the bounce of the dance material. The concentration that moves the last movement forward, even more than its lively tempo, tends to make most other performances seems slightly sluggish.

The next Quartet in this set of recordings is the C-sharp minor, Op. 131, a remarkable work of seven movements, played without pauses. Here Beethoven has recast the sonata cycle into a continuous chain, in which most of the drama and contrast arises from the juxtaposition of the movements rather than during the course of each one; only at the end, in the finale, is full-scale sonata-allegro form used. To make this succeed, the individual movements have rather less internal contrast than is usual with Beethoven.

The first is a slow, very expressive fugue, with an unusual harmonic bias that results from its stressed fourth note; close attention to the fortunes of that note through all its transformations will suggest something of Beethoven's mastery (and also the resourcefulness of the Busch Quartet in carrying out Beethoven's accenting). At the end of the fugue, the music simply lifts up a semitone to the quite distant key of D—a juxtaposition that is surprising but not unprepared, for it had been touched upon in the fugue. This second movement is a gracious dance, in sonata form without a development section, which at one point lands back in C-sharp on the chord that ended the fugue.

Now ensues a brief transition, a discussion that sets up the key of A major for a set of variations; unlike the Adagio of Op. 127, these do not modulate, though the transformations of the theme are almost as remarkable, especially a rapt, hymnlike variation that is punctuated by rude noises from the cello. Finally, in a coda, the theme is tried in other keys (and, briefly, back in A major surrounded by ecstatic trills).

Suddenly the cello makes another rude noise, and we are off on a maniacal, ostensibly simpleminded scherzo that wanders into a harmonic *cul-de-sac* and leads directly into a more tuneful but not very contrasted Trio. This mad whirl repeats a surprising number of times, including an occasion when the Scherzo is played *sul ponticello*—possibly the first use of this device in the standard literature.

The final chord of the Scherzo is immediately contradicted by a vigorous gesture, signaling a new key in which unfolds a simple, solemn Adagio that soon returns to the fugue's key. The seventh movement then begins with its theme of brusque shapes followed by iambic rhythms that rise and fall. This elaborate sonata-form movement incorporates both a theme that explicitly recalls the fugue subject and also a bright passage of descending scales and slow climbing lines. There are many allusions to the keys of the earlier movements, all of which were initially explored in the fugue, and so this driving finale pulls everything together.

Again, the Busch Quartet performance is remarkable for its vivid articulation (for example, in the scales in the last movement that Beethoven marks "non legato," the chiffy, staccato accompaniment to the second of the variations, and the strong accents in the fugue), its intensity (the unremitting drive of the Scherzo), its concern for continuity (the tempo transitions between the variations), and its sonic imagination (the pizzicatos of the witty passage at the end of the Scherzo's Trio).

The final Quartet is at once very much simpler and, in some mysterious way, quite as profound: a very Classical first movement, a vigorous Scherzo full of nervous cross-rhythms, a sublime slow movement, and the blithe final Allegro that follows upon its ominous introduction. This last has a programmatic explanation, decoded by Beethoven at the head of the score: the three notes that begin the introduction ask a question, *"Muss es sein?"* (Must it be?) and their inversion, the main theme of the Allegro, replies *"Es muss sein! Es muss sein!"* (It must be! It must be!). This, and the Busch performance, calls not so much for explication as for attention—and seems an admirable high point on which to end our exploration of great instrumental performances.

The World Records transfers of these recordings are preferable to the German set, which used some inferior source material and has been heavily filtered to remove surface noise, a treatment that detracts from the ensemble's tonal vividness. A second World Records set of the Busch's Beethoven (UK: World Records SHB-27, two disks) includes the Quartets, Op. 59, No. 3, Op. 95, and Op. 132. (The companion to the German set, EMI/Electrola C-181-01822/3, two disks, supplies Op. 59, No. 3, Op. 95, and the first Quartet of Op. 18, as well as Busch and Rudolf Serkin playing the "Spring Sonata.") Not until their first American years did the Busch Quartet record Beethoven's Op. 130, also a fine achievement (UK: CBS 61664), and from the same period comes a good performance of Op. 59, No. 1 (UK: CBS 61888).

All the Schubert recordings by members of the Busch ensembles have recently been packaged (UK: World Records SHB-53, three disks): three String Quartets, including the "Death and the Maiden" and the G major; the Piano Trio in E-flat major, and the Fantasia in C major (this last gloriously played by Busch and Serkin). The "Death and the Maiden" Quartet (US: Turnabout THS-65075) and the Piano Trio (US: Turnabout THS-65064) are also available separately; a much later, less good version of the Piano Trio is also current (US: CBS Odyssey Y-34635).

Equally valuable is a similar compendium of Brahms chamber works (UK: World Records SHB-61, seven disks), containing the first two Piano Quartets and the Piano Quintet (with Serkin), the Clarinet Quintet (with Reginald Kell), the First and Third String Quartets, the first two Violin Sonatas (played by Adolf Busch and Serkin), and the Horn Trio (with Aubrey Brain). The postwar performance of the Third Quartet is disappointing (though certainly worth the attention of connoisseurs), but the rest have been long and justly admired. The two Piano Quartets are available separately: No. 1 in G minor (US: Odyssey Y-34638) and No. 2 in A major (US: Turnabout THS-65061).

Although also celebrated as a soloist, Adolf Busch recorded few concertos. A studio version of the Beethoven, grandly conducted by his older brother Fritz, was never published, although private editions have circulated in recent years; the solo playing is not ideally consistent. The Bach concertos, along with Schumann and Beethoven sonatas, are included in a recent set that mixes studio recordings and concert performances from the American years (US: Odyssey Y3-34639, three disks).

APPENDIX A
Historical Recordings on LP

One way to collect historical recordings is in their original form as 78 RPM disks, and there is still a substantial second-hand market. For most people, however, the bulk, weight, and fragility of shellac records, as well as the inevitable record changes every few minutes, are compelling disadvantages, and they turn to LP reissues. Although something certainly is lost whenever a recording is copied, it is also true that a professional transfer to LP, using the best modern technology, will yield a result more faithful to the original performance than most of us could achieve from the 78 disks without a lot of fancy equipment and engineering skill.

Unfortunately, not all LP transfers are that good. The problems are several. Accidentally or on purpose, many early recordings were made at speeds other than the official 78.26 RPM; an incorrect playing speed will distort pitch, tempo, even tone color. Different groove sizes and shapes were used at different times, and each must be played with the appropriate stylus. In the electrical recording process, bass is reduced to prevent overcutting of the grooves and treble is boosted so that it will end up louder than surface noise, and these modifications must be reversed in playback; such equalization curves varied from one company and period to another.

Defects in the source material can be ameliorated with filters, noise suppressors, and artifical resonance—although, if used carelessly, these can make things worse rather than better. For example, steep filtering of high frequencies will reduce surface noise, but also remove the overtones that give life and color to musical sounds; often enough, the problem could have been solved by locating quieter source material. Once the recording has been copied onto tape, the breaks in the music, at the ends of the 78 RPM sides, must be spliced together as smoothly and naturally as possible.

In recent years, the most consistently successful transfers have been those made for EMI in London by Anthony C. Griffiths, published principally in the HMV ''Treasury'' series and the World Records ''Retrospect'' series—and also, often unidentified, on other EMI labels; the work done by the French, German, and especially the Italian branches of EMI has been on a lower level, and that of RCA, Columbia, and Deutsche Grammophon spotty at best. In Europe, where recordings more than fifty years old are out of copyright, several small labels specialize in historical material; the work of Pearl, in England, has been particularly good recently in the instrumental field. (I have not been able to hear all the alternative editions of the recordings cited in this book, though I have singled out good and poor ones where possible. Some of these recordings would certainly benefit from better transfers than are now available, but I have not excluded any important recording that is fairly decently presented.)

For the most part, the "live" broadcast and concert recordings that circulate, sometimes under, sometimes over the counter, are not considered here. Their general availability is uncertain. Some of them are indeed exceptional from a musical point of view, but far more are of value primarily to historians and to fans who must have everything associated with their idols, creditable or not. In this underground, different editions of the same performance may sound as unlike as night and day; some pirate producers expend time and effort to get the best source material and the best out of it; others just slap any old tape onto a record. *Caveat emptor.*

APPENDIX B

Collecting Historical Recordings

Smaller record shops are not likely to carry many older recordings or the imported labels on which many of them are currently to be found, so the collector outside of the major urban centers is likely to have to depend on ordering by mail. Here is a selected list of dealers who maintain good stocks of such recordings.

UNITED STATES

Darton Records
160 West 56th Street
New York, N.Y. 10019

Discophile, Inc.
26 West 8th Street
New York, N.Y. 10011

King Karol Recordings, Inc.
Box 629
Times Square Station
New York, N.Y. 10036

Liberty Music Shop
417 East Liberty Street
Ann Arbor, Michigan 48104

André Perrault
The Old Stone House
73 East Allen Street
Winooski, Vermont 05404

Serenade Record Shop
1710 Pennsylvania Avenue N.W.
Washington, D.C. 20006

Tower Records
Special Orders (Dept. F)
2525 Jones Street
San Francisco, California 94133

GREAT BRITAIN

Harold Moores Records
2 Great Marlborough Street
London, W. 1

The Music Discount Center, Ltd.
Mail Order Department
47-51 Chalton Street
London NW1 1HY

Tandy's Records Ltd.
24 Islington Row
Birmingham B15 1LJ

Farringdons
28 Holborn Viaduct
London EC1

Templar Record Shops Ltd
9a Irving Street
London WC2

Michael G Thomas
54 Lymington Road
London NW6 1JB